T0361297

E. Y. KUTSCHER

THE LANGUAGE AND
LINGUISTIC BACKGROUND
OF THE ISAIAH SCROLL

(1 Q Is^{a})

INDICES AND CORRECTIONS

STUDIES ON THE TEXTS
OF THE DESERT OF JUDAH

EDITED BY

J. VAN DER PLOEG, O.P.

VOLUME VI A

LEIDEN
E. J. BRILL
1979

E. Y. KUTSCHER

THE LANGUAGE AND LINGUISTIC BACKGROUND OF THE ISAIAH SCROLL (1 Q Is^a)

INDICES AND CORRECTIONS

BY

ELISHA QIMRON

INTRODUCTION BY SHELOMO MORAG

LEIDEN
E. J. BRILL
1979

ISBN 90 04 05974 1

CONTENTS

Introduction by Professor Shelomo Morag   VII

Preface   XI

Bibliography   XIII

The Indices   1

Index of Subjects   3

Indices of Words   15

   Word Index of 1QIs[a]   15

   Word Index of The Thanksgiving Psalms (1QH)   35

   Word Index of the Genesis Apocryphon   36

   Word Index of The Manual of Discipline (1QS)   36

   Word Index of The Order of the War between the Children
     of Light and the Children of Darkness (1QM)   37

   Word Index of Pesher Habakkuk (1QpH)   38

   Word Index of 1QIs[b]   38

   Word Index of other DSS   38

   Word Index of Greek and Latin Transliterations   39

Lists of Corrections   41

   Erroneous Readings in the Hebrew Edition   41

   Corrections to the English Edition   46

INTRODUCTION

Time is perhaps not ripe yet to fully appreciate the contributions made by Eduard Yechezkel Kutscher in the fields of Aramaic and Hebrew. An Aramaist of a towering stature and a Hebraist of no less magnitude, he left his imprint on quite a few fields of study to such an extent, that in these fields one can speak of the pre-Kutscherian period as against the post-Kutscherian period.

Kutscher embarked upon his chosen fields of study with a strong determination to attempt solution of problems and to lay the foundations for a thorough investigation of some rather neglected topics. He was indeed well-equipped for both tasks: his command of the languages involved was masterful; he was completely at home with the texts he investigated; he was well acquainted with adjacent disciplines, such as historical geography, which bordered on his major fields of study; and last but not least, he was able to combine training in traditional philology with methods of modern linguistics.

However, it was not only his erudition that has turned Kutscher into such a leading figure in the field of Aramaic and Hebrew studies. Of no less importance was his vigorous adherence to strict methodology. Kutscher strongly believed in the correct application of appropriate methods: he was convinced that this is the only way to achieve reliable results. In particular, he developed new research methods in Mishnaic Hebrew, Galilean Aramaic, Babylonian Aramaic, and the Hebrew of the Dead Sea Scrolls (primarily the language of the Isaiah Scroll: 1QIs[a]). In all these fields Kutscher laid down new foundations, opened new vistas and established new paths, and achieved a deeper, broader and harmonious understanding of language and text. In spite of his meticulous attention to details, Kutscher never lost hold the general aspects of the problem under investigation; at the same time he managed to integrate the details in a broader frameword and thus to grant them new perspectives.

In his studies of Mishnaic Hebrew, Kutscher established the dictum of the precedence of 'reliable texts', namely, that grammatical studies should, wherever possible, be based on texts which are relatively uncorrupted and which can, therefore, be said to reflect more faithfully the language of the period in question. First in importance among these 'reliable texts' is the *Kaufmann Codex* of the Mishnah. The value of this Codex had already been recognized by some of Kutscher's great predecessors in the field (primarily

H. Yalon and J. N. Epstein), but it took a scholar equipped with Kutscher's philological and linguistic insight to prove that the Ms. is indeed a 'reliable text'. To achieve this he mustered almost all the available evidence from various sources: inscriptions, transcriptions, oral traditions, etc. Due to Kutscher's by now classic studies of the language of the *Kaufmann Codex*, research in Mishnaic Hebrew took on some of the major dimensions of a solid field of work. It is rather uninspiring to consider the fate of Mishnaic Hebrew studies without Kutscher's impact. His contributions have engendered a renaissance in the field.

No less impressive were Kutscher's achievements in Galilean Aramaic. Realizing that the texts previously used for the treatment of this dialect were corrupt, and therefore, linguistically inadequate for proper description, Kutscher set out to find the 'reliable texts' for Galilean Aramaic. He convincingly showed, for the first time, that Mss. such as Ms. Vat. Ebr. 30 of Bereshit Rabba were superior to all others: unlike the printed editions (and some Mss.), these 'reliable texts' are free from the interference of the Aramaic of the Babylonian Talmud. Moreover, they demonstrate intrinsic linguistic traits which definitely establish them as 'reliable texts' for Galilean Aramaic. The relevance of this new approach for this Aramaic dialect cannot be exaggerated.

Kutscher's efforts were also directed towards solving some fundamental problems in the study of Babylonian Aramaic, and although the number of his studies on this field is limited, they are definitely significant. In this case as well, where we have an Aramaic dialect whose available sources have had a turbulent history of transmission that obliterated their linguistic structure, Kutscher contributed fresh insights. As one might well imagine, he was dissatisfied with the linguistic aspects of the text of the Talmud in the printed editions, and, as with Mishnaic Hebrew and Galilean Aramaic, he was able to establish a category of 'reliable texts' and to set up criteria for their identification and testing.

The discovery of the Dead Sea Scrolls and the subsequent publications of the text of the Scrolls, presented scholarship with a great challenge. The significance of the discovery for Jewish History, Biblical Studies, Hebrew Literature, the History of Hebrew and Aramaic and other branches of Jewish studies, soon became apparent, and scholars eagerly took on the demands of the new challenge. Kutscher undertook the task of interpreting, philologically and linguistically, the larger Isaiah scroll (1QIs[a]). The result of his research into the linguistic features of this scroll were presented to the scholarly world in a comprehensive work – *The Language and Linguistic Background of the Isaiah Scroll (1QIs[a])*, which appeared in Hebrew in 1959 and in English in 1974. The merits of this book were justly recognized very soon after its publication. The volume is a composition quite unique in its kind. In addition to a minute analysis of the textual, philological and linguistic features of the scroll, it includes thorough and extensive discussions of major problems in the history of Mishnaic Hebrew and of Middle Aramaic, as well as extensive interpretations of numerous points. However, the interest of the author lies in linguistic phenomenology rather than in scattered details. For Kutscher, the phenomena which typify the language of the Isaiah Scroll are to be regarded as evidence of more general processes which took place within a larger framework and which should be considered in the light of historical circumstances. This approach is exemplified by Kutscher's working hypothesis: in many of the instances where the text of the Scroll departs from the Masoretic Text, this is the result of the interference of Aramaic, as well as the literary (and spoken, in some circles) Hebrew of the first century BC, with the structure of biblical Hebrew. It would be quite natural to assume that such interference did take place. The scribe's Hebrew was centuries remote, in grammar as well as in meaning, from the Classical Hebrew of the biblical period. For members of the scribe's generation such a linguistic situation was rather baffling; it was, therefore, quite natural for the scribe to attempt to make the text of Isaiah as readable as possible for his contemporaries.

Kutscher was able to demonstrate the validity of this hypothesis and showed that the scribe had a rather uninhibited approach to the canonized text of Isaiah and edited it in accordance with the grammatical and lexical norms of his own Hebrew. Not only did the scribe introduce grammatical forms acceptable in his brand of Hebrew though foreign to biblical Hebrew, but he also took the liberty here and there of replacing a rare biblical word, or a word unknown to him, with one more familiar. Through this and similar processes, the text of the Isaiah Scroll came into being.

The riches of the volume are overwhelming. In addition to its being a model of textual criticism, it is virtually a manual for linguistic traits of post-biblical Hebrew and Middle Aramaic. It is doubtless the major study of any definite period in the history of Hebrew to have appeared in this century.

The warm welcome accorded to the Hebrew edition and the recognition of the book's importance, convinced Kutscher of the need to prepare an English translation. For several years he was occupied with planning the translation and, later, with editing the draft. He naturally conceived of the English version as a presentation addressed to a wider circle of readers and had proposed to introduce certain improvements into this version.

However, due to periods of ill-health and his premature death on December 12, 1971, the English edition did not appear exactly as Kutscher would have desired.

Perhaps the greatest defect of the English edition is the lack of indices, which the Hebrew edition has. Dr. Elisha Qimron – a former student of Professor Kutscher's, under whom he began to prepare a doctoral dissertation entitled '*A Grammar of the Hebrew Language of the Dead Sea Scrolls*' (The Hebrew University of Jerusalem, 1976), and a scholar in his own right in the philology of the Dead Sea Scrolls – kindly undertook to remedy this and other shortcomings of the English edition. The results of his work are evident in the present publication.

The significance of the indices is obvious. The subject index, which discloses the immense wealth of Kutscher's *The Language and the Linguistic Background*, will no doubt serve as a working tool for scholars whose interests lie not only in the language of the Isaiah Scroll, but also in the domains of, e.g., *Aramaic, Inscriptions, Late Biblical Books, Mishnaic Hebrew, Samaritan Hebrew and Pentateuch, Greek and Roman Transliterations* (see these entries in the index). The word indices of the Isaiah Scroll and of the other Dead Sea Scrolls (pp. 15-38) greatly facilitate the task of locating Kutscher's discussions of Dead Sea Scrolls Hebrew grammar and semantics.

In addition to the indices the present publication also includes two lists of *corrigenda*, the first consisting of corrections (primarily – presentations of preferred readings) to the Hebrew edition, while the second contains corrections to the English edition.

The present publication, which is intended to serve as a supplement to the *Language and Linguistic Background of the Isaiah Scroll*, will certainly increase the value of the English version of this great work, and should provide a key for its use by scholars and students alike. This is definitely in keeping with our memory of the spirit of its late author, who was not only a deeply devoted scholar but was also completely committed to the dissemination of learning, especially among younger scholars, whose progress was always of major concern to him.

SHELOMO MORAG
Professor of Hebrew

The Hebrew University of Jerusalem
December 1978

PREFACE

The late Professor Kutscher's Hebrew book, *The Language and Linguistic Background of the Isaiah Scroll* [= *1QIsᵃ*], published in 1959, is the most important contribution so far to the study of the language of this Scroll in particular, and of the language of the Dead Sea Scrolls [= *DSS*] in general. Moreover, in this study the author does not restrict himself to the *DSS* but deals with all the sources in Hebrew and in Aramaic dialects which have a bearing on *1QIsᵃ*. These include the late biblical books, the Babylonian vocalization, the Greek and Latin transliterations, Mishnaic Hebrew, the Samaritan tradition, Palestinian Aramaic, the spoken Aramaic of Ma'lūla and the colloquial Arabic of Palestine. Kutscher's research is indeed a comprehensive and sound linguistic study of the major aspects of the Hebrew of the Second Temple period and its history, and particulary of the problem of the coexistence of Hebrew and Aramaic during this period.

The author's main thesis, now proved beyond any doubt, is that *1QIsᵃ* is an example of a vulgar text dating from the Second Temple period. Its language shows features – hitherto unattested – which result from the influence both of the spoken Hebrew and of the spoken Aramaic of the Jews of that period. The problems of the Biblical text in general and of the book of Isaiah in particular receive a thorough treatment. One cannot deal seriously with the textual problems in Isaiah without having recourse to Kutscher's study.

Fifteen years after the appearance of the Hebrew edition, E. J. Brill of Leiden, published an English translation. This is an important contribution to the study of the Bible and the Hebrew language, since it makes Kutscher's research methods available to a wide circle of scholars who have no access to the Hebrew original.

The advantage of the English edition over the Hebrew original lies in the fact that the *corrigenda* and *addenda* of the latter were incorporated into the former in their appropriate places. The English edition, however, suffers from two shortcomings, which are due to the ill-health of the author while preparing the book and his premature death:

1. Lack of indices, which greatly reduces the practical value of the work.

2. A considerable number of misprints, especially in the case of Hebrew words.

The aim of the present composition is to correct the above mentioned deficiencies. It contains an index of subjects, indices of words and forms, and lists of corrections, including corrections of mistakes in the Hebrew edition which have not been eliminated in the English edition.

I consider it a privilege to make this modest contribution to my late teacher's great work.

E. Q.

BIBLIOGRAPHY

The list includes reviews of Kutscher's book, as well as books and articles containing suggestions for more correct readings in *1QIs*ᵃ. Abbreviations of the bibliographical items are given in square brackets.

1. I. Garbell, 'On the Language of the Isaiah Scroll', *Lešonenu*, 26 (1962), pp. 140–146 (Review; Hebrew).

2. M. Greenberg, *JBL*, 79 (1960), pp. 278–280 (Review).

3. K.G. Kuhn, *Konkordanz zu den Qumrantexten*, Göttingen, 1960 [= Kuhn].

4. D. Leibel, 'The Isaiah Scroll of Qumrān and its Language', *Molad*, 17 (1958/59), pp. 450–452 (Review; Hebrew).

5. D.S. Loewinger, 'Remnants of a Hebrew Dialect in *1QIs*ᵃ', *Essays on the Dead Sea Scrolls in Memory of E. L. Sukenik*, Jerusalem, 1961, pp. 141–161 (Hebrew) [= Loewinger].

6. Id., VT, 4 (1954), pp. 80–87.

7. S. Morag, *Kirjath Sefer,* 36 (1960/61), pp. 24–32 (Review; Hebrew).

8. E. Qimron, 'The Distinction between *Waw* and *Yod* in the Qumran Documents', *Beit Miqra,* 52 (1973), pp. 102–112 (Hebrew) [= Qimron, *Waw* and *Yod*].

9. Id., 'Initial *Alef* as a Vowel Letter in Hebrew and Aramaean Documents From Qumran Compared With Other Hebrew and Aramaean Sources', *Lešonenu*, 39 (1975), pp. 133–146 (Hebrew) [Qimron, Initial *Alef*].

10. S. Segert, *Ar. Or.*, 29 (1961), pp. 685–687 (Review).

11. R. Tournay, *RB*, 67 (1960), pp. 437–438 (Review).

12. M. Wallenstein, *JSS*, 7 (1962), pp. 116–119 (Review).

13. H. Yalon, *Studies in the Dead Sea Scrolls — Philological Essays* (1949–1952), Jerusalem 1967 (Hebrew) [= Yalon].

THE INDICES

The indices consist of: 1) index of subjects, 2) word and form indices similar to those of the Hebrew edition. The major word index is that of words and forms in *1QIs^a*. To this we have added indices of words appearing in other *DSS* and dealt with in the book, as well as of Hebrew words in Greek and Latin transliteration.

The subject index also includes words from Mishnaic Hebrew and other Semitic languages which have been mentioned in the book in connection with the *DSS*. In most cases only the number of the page is indicated, and only words which have specifically been dealt with are explicitly pointed out. Comprehensive entries such as Mishnaic Hebrew are arranged in the following order: general subjects, spelling, phonology, morphology, syntax and lexicology. The entry *Aramaic* includes the various Aramaic dialects in the following order: first, groups of dialects, and then the various dialects arranged historically. Subjects which appear in the notes are indicated by a capital N after the page number. Each subject is mentioned only once even if it appears several times on the same page.

The word indices are arranged alphabetically: the verbs according to roots, and the nouns according to their basic forms. In this matter we have deviated from the practice adopted in the Hebrew edition where the index is arranged according to forms. We have considered an arrangement by roots more practical. Only in those cases where the form of the word in the Scroll is difficult and the root not unequivocal has the word been listed both according to its root (according to Kutscher's conclusion or to the best of my understanding) and to its form in the book.

The word indices also contain forms such as the pronominal suffix ‑כנה in ברגליכנה etc. Verbal forms or noun patterns appear under the root קטל.

The word index of *1QIs^a* does not include the lists which appear at the end of the book according to the sequence of chapters in the book of Isaiah. These are:

Interchanges in the definite article 411, *waw* conjunctive 414 ff., *Ketib* and *Qere* 519 ff., *Madinḥa'e* and *Ma'arbha'e* 521 ff., Suspended Letters and Words 522 ff., Erasures etc. 531 ff., Words not in MT 536 ff., Words in MT lacking in the Scroll 547 ff., Additions 555 ff., Change of Persons, 556 ff., Different Word Order 563 ff.

Corrections of readings in the Hebrew edition are given in the indices in square brackets, following the reading given in the book, e.g. כאיב [= כאוב]. Misprints in the English edition, however, are not recorded in the indices; only the correct form is given. Forms not found as such in the Scroll are marked by an asterisk (*).

INDEX OF SUBJECTS

a

Semitic long *a* 473

a → *o*

in closed unaccented syllable 482–483N

Abstract noun

indicating the plural 370

Accentuation 40–41, 110, 196, 333–337, 338, 339, 465

Accusative 383, 410, 414

Additions

∼ in the margins, 522–531; ∼ in the Scroll, 536–547; ∼ by another hand, 555–556

Adverbs 52, 413–414

Afformatives, see: Suffixes

Agreement, see: Congruence

Akkadian

∼ clash with Aramaic, 13–14; Aramaic influence on ∼ 14, 27; ∼ loan word in Greek and Latin, 475; ∼ transliteration of Phoenician, 436; final vowels, 436; ∼ ḥ signifying Aramaic-Hebrew ע, 119; personal pronouns, 435, 438; various patterns, 463, 483N, 487; position of the apposition, 429; various words, 224, 228, 232, 239, 255, 317, 318, 374, 459, 460, 475, 478, 479, 486; proper nouns, 96, 99, 102, 104–105, 113, 116, 120, 123, 227, 412, 456; ∼ letters from *Ta'nak*, 367, 423

Akkadian, see also: Inscriptions

Aleph, see: Spelling, Glide, Gutturals, Omission

Alliteration 253

Allophone 491, 492

Analogy

∼ in personal pronouns and pronominal suffixes, 435, 438, 439, 448, 450; various words, 174, 197, 200, 451, 458

Ancient forms, see: Archaic

Apodosis, see: Textual influence

Apposition 427, 429

Arabia

dialect of ∼ 205

Arabic

Hebrew, Aramaic substratum in ∼ 493; ∼ influence on Aramaic, 26, 439; ∼ influence on the Masoretes, 45, 442; *u → i* in ∼ dialects, 54, 452, 472, 489–494; *ā → ō*, 495–496; final *mem/nun*, 60, 518; final vowels, 436; pronouns and pronominal suffixes with final *a*, 50, 435, 437, 438, 449–450; three forms of the perfect, 465; imperfect used for infinitive, 330, 430; Hebrew-Aramaic words, 16, 67, 201, 337, 479, 480, 488, 516N; various words, 32, 34, 69N, 70, 81N, 115, 143, 201, 232, 234, 237, 242, 245, 251, 255, 256, 265, 277, 279, 282, 283, 286, 288, 291, 294, 377, 382, 450, 454, 456–460, 462, 473, 478, 479, 480, 483N, 486, 496, 497, 506

ARAMAIC

∼ as *lingua franca*, 9; the dominant language in Jerusalem, 89; the ∼ of the Scribe, 30; Hebrew influence on ∼ 14, 15, 187, 188, 477; ∼ clash with Akkadian, 13–14; Akkadian imprint upon ∼ 14; ∼ form in substandard Hebrew, 63; Hebrew read as ∼ 175; ∼ words in Josephus, 12, 24, 90; ∼ words in the Gospels, 12, 90; ∼ meaning ascribed to Hebrew word in the Septuagint, 75; ∼ words in Arabic, 59, 67, 488; ∼ influence on Arabic, 496; ∼ elements in the Scroll, 187–215; ∼ influence and Aramaisms, 23–30, 46, 64, 88, 150, 184N, 187–192, 219, 229, 274, 288, 313, 327, 344, 351, 362, 370, 371, 372, 375, 376, 377, 399, 409, 442, 450, 451, 453, 481–482, 566; the spelling ואֿ, 173–174; *yod* representing final *e*, 158; the spelling מקֿ טל (instead of מקוטל) not an Aramaism, 140–142; תֿ in the plural suffix not an

Aramaism, 134–135; ~ influence in the spellings of the Nash papyrus, 84; *plene* spelling to prevent ~ pronunciation, 19, 20, 184; the weakening of the gutturals not an ~ trait, 59; ~ pronunciation in Hebrew, 250; the accentuation of the Segolates, 110; definite article, 90, 368; various forms, 77, 337N, 343, 347; various patterns, 205–206, 365, 368, 374, 483, 502–503; position of the apposition, 429; active participle used as passive, 350; imperfect used for infinitive, 430; various words, 37, 69N, 81N, 92, 93, 162–163, 191, 222, 223, 233, 234, 240, 245, 247, 251, 253, 256, 257, 261, 262, 265, 272, 282, 285, 289, 293, 294, 307, 310, 376, 379, 398, 403N, 410, 459, 464, 496; place names, 12

Aramaic dialects
מהקטל in ~ 24, 72; *qutl* pattern, 68; *u* → *i*, 54, 452; היה before pl., 400; various words, 228, 384

Eastern Aramaic
qutl pattern, 201; its accentuation, 338, 339

Western Aramaic
its origin and internal divisions, 10–11; ~ having superseded Hebrew, 12–13; Hebrew traits in ~ 15; its accentuation, 338; weakening of the gutturals, 58, 510; influence of the labials and *resh*, 56; קטל(י) → קטול(י), 342; *qutl* pattern, 201; קטול used in ~ 475; the pronominal suffix כי-, 211–212

Jewish Aramaic 187, 479
Palestinian Aramaic 70, 267, 456

Ancient Aramaic
~ containing no hint of the weakening of the gutturals, 59; *heh* of *haph‘el*, 72, 198; the word כביר, 246

Official Aramaic
the official language of the Persian empire, 9, 12; the offshoots of ~ 10; dissimilation in ~ 515; various words, 211, 215, 290

Biblical Aramaic
representation of final *e*, 158; influence of the labials and *resh*, 496; *u* → *i*, 478–479; glide, 516; *yod* → *aleph*, 513; *heh*

of *haph‘el*, 72, 198; כי-, אתי in ~ 190, 208, 211; 3rd pers. fem. afformative of the perfect, 192; the ending -ות, 383; קטול pattern, 203; קטלון/קטלן pattern, 205; plural forms like עממיא, 372; various words, 201, 233, 385, 477

Nabataean
an offshoot of Official Aramaic, 10; proper nouns with final *u*, 120; *heh* of *haph‘el*, 198–199; ~ inscriptions, 152

Palmyrene
an offshoot of Official Aramaic, 10; spelling in ~ inscriptions, 152, 153; the spelling לוא, 173; spelling ראישיא רש, 177; *a* → *o*, 495; *u* → *i*, 493; final *mem/nun* interchange, 61; *heh* of *haph‘el*, 198–199; בריך שמה an epithet of a certain deity, 38, 226; various words, 252, 329, 390

Aramaic of the *Targumim*
its origin, 486; as descendent of Official Aramaic, 10; the vowel *u*, 486; pronominal suffixes and perfect afformatives, 192, 212, 477; *quttul* pattern, 487; *qutl* pattern, 201; יה-, 123; various words, 206, 230, 233, 252, 455N, 458–460, 478, 479, 480, 486; place names, 97, 101, 102

Galilean Aramaic
~ texts influenced by Babylonian Aramaic, 485; final *aleph/heh*, 164; *yod* representing final *e*, 158; *nun* added in final position, 121; its accentuation, 339; assimilation of *taw*, 346; *u* → *i*, 485; influence of the labials and *resh*, 497; pronunciation of the *shewa*, 498, 500, 501; weakening of the gutturals, 510; *yod* → *aleph*, 513N; glide, 516; יקטל → יקטול, 39; *heh* of *haph‘el*, 198; קטול pattern, 203; pl. forms like עממין, 372; various words, 201, 259, 324, 329, 390, 460, 482, 484

Christian Aramaic
spelling in ~ 153; *aleph* as medial vowel letter, 162; final *aleph*, 164; various spellings, 187, 188, 258; pronunciation of the *shewa*, 56, 498, 500, 501; glide, 516; weakening of the gutturals, 510; influence of the labials and *resh*, 497; *yod* → *aleph*, 513N; auxiliary vowels,

337N; *u* → *i*, 483–485; its accentuation, 339; יקטל → יקטול, 39; *heh* of *haph'el*, 198; יקטולן a Hebraism in ~ 40, 338; the pronominal suffix כי-, 27, 211; קטלתי, in ~ from Syriac, 190; אתי/את, 208–209; pl. forms like עממין, 372; various patterns, 53, 54, 68, 202, 205, 476, 503; various words, 57, 70, 111, 114, 201, 204, 206, 244N, 251, 272, 280, 329, 360, 367, 374, 376, 379, 381, 387, 390, 458, 459, 460, 479, 481, 482, 483N, 485, 486, 511

Samaritan Aramaic
weakening of the gutturals, 509–510; loss of voice in final position, 517; *shwa* before labials and *resh*, 498; assimilation of *taw*, 346; *heh* of *haph'el*, 198; קטול pattern, 203; various words, 61, 98, 233, 280, 329, 500, 513

Babylonian Aramaic
influence on Galilean Aramaic texts, 485; *aleph* as medial vowel letter, 162; *aleph* as final vowel letter, 164; the gutturals, 81, 509–510; its accentuation, 41; various words, 379, 455N, 456, 460

Mandaic
plene spelling, 7; *aleph* as medial vowel letter, 162; weakening of the gutturals, 509–510; קטלן / קטל pattern, 205N; various words, 187, 479, 500

Syriac
waw as vowel letter, 7; final *aleph*, 164; *u* → *i*, 479–480; *ā* → *ō* in western ~ 495; its accentuation, 41; personal pronouns, pronominal suffixes and perfect affromatives, 23, 25, 27, 208, 211, 290; various patterns, 205N, 475, 487; various words, 3, 127, 143, 188, 206, 228, 230, 233, 246, 261, 272, 294, 329, 367, 372, 375, 377, 379, 403N, 455N, 456, 458, 459, 460, 462, 475, 478, 480N, 482, 485, 486, 488, 515; modern ~ 480, 486

Ma'lula
its accentuation, 41; the gutturals, 59, 510; *u* → *i*, 488–489; *ā* → *ō*, 495; יקטל → יקטול, 39; various topics, 3, 16, 81N

Aramaic of Tur Abdin 438–439

Aramaic, see also: Elephantine papyri, Inscriptions

Archaic
~ pronominal forms in the Scroll, 192, 434, 435, 436, 439, 448, 449, 450; ~ features in the Scroll, 54, 62, 332, 476; replacement of ~ forms, 193, 324–325; ~ words and forms renewed at a late period, 25, 26, 27, 68, 190, 209

Archaism
in Biblical Hebrew, 191, 232; in the Nash papyrus, 84, 184N; intended ~ 325, 390

Article
definite ~ 206, 240, 376, 411–412

Assimilation
methodological notes, 256, 457; intervocalic ~ 113, 476, 484; ~ of a vowel to a consonant, 114, 194, 202, 492, 496–498; ~ of consonants, 345–346, 511; ~ of word pairs, 97, 227, 253, 270, 381

Assimilation, see also: Labials and *Resh*

Asverus, see: Scroll

Asyndetic
~ relative clause, 349, 431–432

Atomistic
~ exegetical method, 34–35, 262, 265, 313

Attraction
~ of spellings, 182

Babylonian Vocalization
preservation of the vowel *u*, 54, 65, 464–467, 472–473, 478; the forms of the imperfect, 196, 332, 334, 336N; pronominal suffixes, 46, 47, 446; perfect afformative, 45; various patterns, 458, 459, 460, 471; various words, 374, 387, 458, 462, 481, 482, 483, 492

Back formation 369, 463, 515

Bar-Kochba Letters
spellings in ~ 151, 159, 167, 185, 440, 510; the form גללאים, 514

Basic Biblical Hebrew 29 ff.

Ben-Sira 219

Bet essentiæ 373

Blend 222, 249, 259, 265, 312–313, 376, 390

Calque 377

Canaanite
defective spelling of the ~ inscriptions, 6; *u* → *i*, 453; *a* → *o*, 366; *nun* added in the pronominal suffix, 445–446; *quttui*

pattern, 487; various words, 97, 453, 511

Case endings, 387; see also: (final) Vowels

Chronicles, see: Late Biblical books

Classical Biblical Hebrew 4, 5, 8, 327

Cluster
breakup of a ~ of two consonants, 336N

Codex, see: Scroll

Cohortative 39–40, 326–327, 330, 332, 340

Coins
spelling on ~ 5, 107, 133–134, 147, 153–154, 167; the suffix יה־, 4

Collective nouns
followed by singular, 401; followed by plural, 398, 399

Colloquial
contemporary ~ Hebrew 288, 327

Communities
pronunciation traditions of the Jewish ~ 18, 40, 41, 47, 48, 65, 66, 67, 333, 334, 336, 339, 340, 509–510

Conflation of readings 236, 262, 289, 314, 534, 542, 544, 545, 563

Congruence
~ in gender and number, 244, 273, 280, 305, 319; in relative clause, 430

Conjugation 234, 358–365, 469

Construct State
~ before the preposition, 429; ~ instead of apposition, 429

Contamination, see: Blend

Copyists
~ of the *Mishnah* 339

Corrections
~ in the Scroll 531–536

Daleth
final ~ pronounced as *taw* 227, 265, 517

Date
~ of Biblical manuscripts, 1–2; of the Scroll, 55, 71–73, 198–199, 423; of the *u → i* change, 469

Dialect(s)
of the Scroll, 50, 51, 52, 54, 55, 61, 62, 72, 106, 109, 140, 142, 196, 205, 230, 294, 314, 332, 333, 365, 374, 376, 387, 435, 436–439, 446, 449, 450, 474, 476, 477, 531; Hebrew ~ 45, 65–67, 339; ~ in the Bible, 64; Jerusalem ~ 89–95; Judaean ~ 95; northern Hebrew ~ 211;

the ~ of Arabia, 205; Hebrew-Aramaic ~ current in palestine, 207

Dialectical changes   72

Dialectical forms   325

Dialectical variations
~ in the transliterations   62–63

Diminutives   479

Diphthongs   51, 64

Dissimilation   53, 98N, 206, 256, 282, 452, 453, 454–458, 461, 467–471, 473–477, 479, 480, 481, 482, 484, 485, 492, 511–515

Dittography   222, 257, 382, 422, 538, 540, 542, 545

Doublet
Hebrew-Aramaic ~ 282

Dura Europus
spellings in ~ papyrus 136, 168

El-Amarna letters
dissimilation (*u → i*), 53, 453, 454, 469, 473; *a → o*, 495; final vowels in ~ 436; preformative *taw* in the 3rd pers. masc. pl. of the imperf., 325; the pronominal suf. -*mu*, 49–50; various words and forms, 3, 69, 110N, 169, 181, 376

Elephantine papyri
written in Official Aramaic, 10; spelling in the ~ 153; *aleph* as medial vowel letter, 20, 161; *yod* representing final *e*, 158; interchanging of final *aleph heh*, 164; personal pronouns, pronominal suffixes and perfect afformatives, 25, 27, 190, 208, 211, 447; *heh* of *haph'el*, 72, 198; pl. forms like עממין, 372; the ending ־ות, 383–384; ־יהו/־יה, 4, 123; imperfect used for infinitive, 430; כהל ~ imperfect, 330; various words, 24, 187, 204, 230, 233, 251N, 274; proper nouns, 96, 111, 113

Emphatic consonants   489

Emphatic state, see: Article

Endings
־אות/־יות, 207, 389; ־ות, 200, 383; ־ָן, 365, 379

Endings, see also: Suffixes

Error
mechanical ~ 221, 227, 228, 229, 237, 242, 245, 249, 250, 255, 270, 272, 273, 285, 286, 293, 294, 306, 313, 354, 359, 363, 385, 403, 406, 408

Ethiopic 435

Eusebius
proper nouns 69–70, 98

Eusebius Onomasticon 61

Evolution
~ of textual substitution 310

Exegetical substitution 220, 222, 230, 313, 319, 384, 401, 406

Exegetical tradition
~ in the Versions 306

Expanded
~ forms in medial *waw* verbs 342

Final
ם or ך followed by ה 451

Final מ 88, 91

First Temple Period, 123; see also: Classical Biblical Hebrew

Forms
special ~ of medial *waw* verbs, 39, 234, 254, 381; ~ of tertiary *heh* verbs, 342–343; dual ~ 388; ־כה/ך־, 447; secondary ~ 435; misc. ~ 344; substitution of ~ 315–346

Frequency
plene spelling in common words, 138–139, 210; ~ of המה־ in short words, 450

Fricatives 489

Gaonic literature
plene spelling, 7; the verb סתר in *qal*, 150

Geminate verbs 321, 344

Gender 43–44, 392–394, 431

Gentilic suffix 38–39, 112, 399, 512–515

Glide 84, 181N, 203, 490, 515–516

Gloss 537

Gospels
Aramaic ~ 204

Greek
~ spoken by Jews, 11, 12, 13, 89; Hebrew of speakers of ~ 70, 195, 510–511; ~ influence on Hebrew, 59–60; ~ words in Christian Aramaic, 484; Akkadian word in ~ 475; nomenclature for clothes in Mishnaic Hebrew, 288; Latin and ~ influence on Punic, 7; various words, 475, 479, 481, 484

Gutturals
weakening of the ~ 57–60, 84, 87, 88, 91–94, 98, 102, 108, 112, 122, 151, 175, 195, 206, 220, 221, 229, 241, 245, 247, 251, 253, 254, 258, 260, 264, 273, 277, 287, 289, 292, 345, 347, 368, 377, 390, 392–393, 401, 408, 410, 412, 498–502, 505–511, 516, 531

Hapax legomena 310, 317–319, 366, 369, 372, 379, 389

Ḥaṭeph 339–340

Hebrew
knowledge of ~ in the period of the Versions 308

Heh
~ as medial vowel letter 199N; ~ as final vowel letter, 22, 158–159, 164, 182–184; ~ of *hiph'il*, 24, 72, 198

Hendiadys 410

Hiatus 516

Hiph'il
primary *yod* verbs, 201; active participle and imperfect of ~ with *heh*, 24, 72, 198; Aramaic forms, 197; various forms, 345

Historic orthographical development 186

Hithpa'el
the *taw* of ~ 345, 346

Homiletic interpretation 75, 100, 181N, 282, 289, 291, 296, 313, 315, 322, 364, 365, 366, 369, 375, 378, 561, 562

Homoeoteleuton 548, 549, 550, 552, 554

Hybrid forms 243, 309, 325, 326, 381, 451

Hypercorrection 28, 61, 106, 202 234, 327, 463, 477, 480N, 492, 499, 515

Ideograms
spelling in the Parsik and Pehlevi ~ 15, 22, 24, 168, 174, 176–177, 185, 187, 188

Idiosyncrasies 337

Imitation
~ of neighbouring languages 221, 387, 445

Imperative
instead of other verbal forms, 348, 508; the form of the ~ of *qal*, 193–197; *u – i* vowels in the ~ of *qal*, 464, 467, 470, 478; the long form of the ~ 464–465; ~ in Gal. Aram., 485; correspondence between the ~ and the imperfect form, 196

Imperfect
its use in the Scroll, 352–357; the form of the ~ of *qal*, 335; ~ with prono-

minal suffixes, 331, 336–337N, 339–340;
~ used for infinitive, 330, 430; correspondence between the ~ and the imperative form, 196; the form יקטלה, 328;
short forms, 328
Imperfect lengthened, see: Cohortative
Impersonal subject 44, 360, 401–403
Inconsistency
~ of the spelling in the Scroll 141–142,
146
Indefinite 256
Indefinite personal subject, see: Impersonal
subject
Infinitive
~ absolute, 269; with or without בכל״ם,
41, 321, 322, 346–348; the vowels of
the ~ of qal, 465–467; ~ denoting command, 347; ~ and the imperfect, 288;
~ replaced by other verbal forms, 358,
508; hiph'il ~ without heh, 39, 345;
special forms of the ~ 39, 200, 324, 345,
374, 455, 477; ~ instead of לָשֶׁבַּת, 316,
375
Inscription(s)
yod representing short i, 158; double yod
representing consonantal yod, 160; aleph
instead of final heh, 163; the spelling
זוא, 173; the spellings of מחנים, 187;
the spelling תה־, 442; various spellings
in the Hebrew ~ 7, 24, 129, 133, 147,
148N, 153, 155, 158; spellings of the
Aramaic ~ 6–7, 136, 147, 148, 153, 155,
161; the vocalization of the word רבי,
65N; הית in the Siloam ~ 191, 343;
the Lachish letters, 4, 7, 123, 351;
weakening of the gutturals in the Jerusalem ~ 92–93; various features, 61, 64,
123, 469–470; various words and forms
in the Jerusalem ~ 104N, 105, 339, 501;
Hebrew ~ from Jerusalem, 90; Egyptian ~ 3; Aramaic ~ 9, 12, 90, 290;
various words and forms in the Aramaic ~ 3–5, 96, 102, 108; Assyrian ~
380, 453, 454, 495
Inscriptions Assyrian, see also: Akkadian
Interchange
i – u ~ 106; qameṣ – o ~ 247; sin/
samech ~ 88; ~ of the pharyngeals in
Galilean Aramaic, 250; daleth/resh ~
260; final mem/nun ~ 91, 94, 296

Intransitive verbs, 39, 194, 323, 340–341;
see also: Neutral verbs
Intransitive meaning
~ of hiph'il 363

Jerusalem
the dialect of ~ 89–95, 339

Kimchi 243, 276, 278, 279, 293, 391
Ktibh 519–521
Kulturkampf
Hebrew-Aramaic ~ 73

Labials and resh
influence of the ~ 56, 63, 118, 121, 122,
194, 202, 375, 450, 459, 464, 470, 473,
474, 475, 480N, 482N, 484, 496–497
Lachish letters, see: Inscriptions
Lamed
influence of ~ 480
Language(s)
~ in conflict, 13; ~ of the Hellenized
part of the population, 59–60, 70;
~ spoken in Jerusalem, 90; influence of
a living ~ on the Scroll, 313
Laryngeals, see: Gutturals
Late Biblical books
~ and the Scroll, 15, 314; final aleph/
heh interchange, 164; the spelling יא־,
180; the spelling וא־, 173; the spelling
דויד, 5, 99; final mem/nun interchange,
61; the form of the imperfect, 193, 326,
327; הם/המה־, 434; the ending יה־, 5, 123;
the gentilic suffix, 514; the form חזקיה(ו),
104; position of the apposition, 429–430;
infinitive denoting command, 347; impersonal subject, 401–402; waw conjunctive, 422; waw consecutive, 351; double
plural in the contract state, 399; collective nouns, 398; the construction יום
ויום, 423; את in Chronicles, 413; various
words, 113, 115, 204, 207, 233, 247, 252,
266, 268, 276, 283, 288, 372, 378, 385,
386, 390, 391, 400, 407; דרמשק, 3–4
Late Biblical Hebrew
~ features in the Scroll, 29 ff., 62; כי־
current in ~ 212
Late poetry
the form אקטלה 327
Latin
~ and Greek influence on Punic 7; Akkadian word in ~ 475

Liquids 256

Loan words or elements

Hebrew-Aramaic ~ in Arabic, 16, 67, 201, 377, 479, 480, 488, 516N; Aramaic ~ in Hebrew, 24–28, 187–215; Hebrew ~ in Aramaic, 14–15, 187, 188, 338, 447; Aramaic ~ in Akkadian, 14, 27; Akkadian ~ in Aramaic, 14; Greek ~ in Hebrew-Aramaic, 288, 481, 484; Semitic ~ in Greek and Latin, 455, 459, 475

Local tradition

~ of inscriptions 96

Letter of Aristeas 470

Locative הֵ‑ 91N 413–414

Logograms, see: Ideograms

Ma'arbha'e 521–522

Madinḥa'e 521–522

Ma'lūla, see: Aramaic

Mandaic, see: Aramaic

Manuscripts

of the Bible, 1–2, 77; of the Septuagint, 2

Masoretes 442, 492, 510

Meaning 239, 241, 243–245. 263, 264, 281, 284, 382, 385, 391, 422–423, 427 et al.

Megilat Ta'anit

written in Official Aramaic 10, 12

Mem

dissimilatory ~ 515; final ~ 88, 91, 451; final *mem/nun* interchange, 61, 518

Metathesis 256, 285, 288, 346

Midrashic literature

נוסנא in the ~ 24

Mishnaic Hebrew

editing of ~ texts, 8; development of ~ 9; ~ as a spoken language, 12; ~ superseded by Aramaic and Greek, 13; preservation of ~ by the common people, 13; as product of Hebrew-Aramaic clash, 15; Aramaic influence on ~ 29; ~ and the Scroll, 30, 32–44; the spelling of the word כהן, 129; the spelling of the afformative תָ‑, 441; ‑וא‑ ‑או‑ as medial vowel letters for *o*, 20, 166–168; *yod* representing final *e*, 158; *aleph* as medial vowel letter, 162; final *aleph/heh* interchange, 164; the spelling הא‑, 448; the spelling ירושלים, 5; the spelling לוא, 173; the spelling of the word רושם, 22, 168,

171; *sin/samech* interchange, 185; the *shwa* pronounced as the following vowel, 501; כילו (= כאילו), 500; *yod* → *aleph*, 513N; glide, 516; *u* → *i*, 481–483; *a* followed by labials or *resh* → *o*, 56; weakening of the gutturals in Jerusalem, 93–94; final added *nun*, 121; accentuation, 335; pronouns and pronominal suffixes, 27, 46–48, 51, 212, 392, 434–435, 447; the forms of the imperfect, the imperative and the infinitive, 193, 195, 324, 327, 328, 329, 340, 342, 343, 393–394; pausal forms, 333–336, 338; the form קְטַל, 341; the geminate verbs, 344; conjugations, 140, 234, 322, 344, 362; *heh* of *hiph'il*, 198, 345; tertiary *heh* verbs, 190, 191, 343; infinitive, 321, 346, 347, 430; קְטוֹל pattern, 203; the plural ending ‑אות, ‑יות, 207, 389; the ending וֹת, 200; the ending ‑יה, 4, 123; סדיקין כריכין etc., 379; the tenses in ~ 41–42, 350, 351; impersonal subject, 402; asyndetic relative clause, 320, 431; the apposition, 429; passive participle, 350; מי followed by plural, 397; the particle את, 413; prepositions, 410; לא, 19, 250; סודמי etc., 111; the word נמתי, 451; various words, 3, 24, 57, 63, 70, 75, 150, 201, 217, 219, 220, 224, 227, 228, 232, 233, 234, 239–242, 245, 246, 247, 251, 252, 253, 258–261, 263, 264, 265, 269, 271, 272, 273, 275, 276, 277, 280–283, 285, 286, 289–293, 295, 307, 310, 316–319, 323, 324, 344, 358, 359, 361–364, 366, 367, 368, 370–376, 381–391, 394, 400, 402, 404, 405, 408, 414, 456, 457, 459, 474, 480, 485, 486, 511, 515, 557

Model texts 77 ff.

Moods 346–358

Nabataean, see: Aramaic

Nash papyrus

its date, 2; its spelling, 129; the spelling of יקטל, 136; the spelling לוא, 87, 173; the spelling of the third pers. sing. pron. afformative, 184N

Negative

repeating the ~ 431

Negative particle

~ לא with the participle 349 430–431

Neutral verbs, 320, 341, 349, 465; see also: Intransitive verbs

Nippur tablets

יהו/־יה ־ 123

Nisbe, see: Gentilic suffix

Nomen unitatis 240

Northern dialect of Biblical Hebrew

קטלתי sec. pers. fem. sing., 190N; ־כי sec. pers. fem. sing. suf., 211

Number

change in grammatical ~ 43, 291, 388–389, 394–401, 431

Nun

final *mem/nun* interchange, 61, 518; final added ~ 94, 121

O

o instead of *qameṣ, pataḥ* and *segol* 247, 473–474

Omission

~ of final *resh*, 237; ~ of *aleph*, 292; ~ of *nun*, 292

Opposition

semantic ~ 468–469, 491–492

Order

changed word ~ 563–564

Orthography, see: Spelling

Orthographic convention 514

Palestinian vocalization

pronominal suffixes and afformatives of the perfect, 45, 46, 47, 446; differing somewhat from the Tiberian, 65

Palmyrene, see: Aramaic

Papyri 2, 77, 78, 105, 140, 470

Paraphrases

~ in Chronicles 73

Partiality

~ of the scribe to the root אתה 222

Particles 389–392, 412–413

Participle 72, 85, 127–130, 198, 277, 349, 350

Parts of the Scroll 104, 140, 180, 181, 182, 184, 210, 242, 256, 321, 326, 327, 365, 384, 391, 434, 446–449, 564–566

Passive

~ participle, 129–130, 277, 350; ~ *qal*, 344, 361, 362, 364; expressing impersonal subject, 401–402

Pattern(s)

~ substitution, 365–386; existing morphological ~ absorbing a new creation, 467–468; *quṭl* ~ 201–203, 238, 390, 476, 478, 502–504; *qaṭl* ~ 390, 477; קטלה/קטלה, 203; ~ קטול 470–471, 477; קטלן/קטלן ~ 205–206, 455, 469–470; the segolate ~ 458–462; קוטלן/קטלן (in Christian Aramaic), 484; קְטֵל → קָטֵל in the construct state, 462; קְטֵל ~ 454, 463; *quṭṭul* ~ 480, 481, 487; קטול/קטול in Christian Aramaic, 484–485; /קוטלן קטלן ~ 483N; מקלה/מקלה/מקלה ~ 462–463; קטול ~ 455, 475; קטול ~ 455, 475

Pausal forms 40–41, 154, 194–195, 330–340

Perfect 352–358, 465

Persons

confusions of grammatical ~ 189

Pharyngeals, see: Gutturals

Phoenician

כ (= כי), 180; *u → i*, 54, 452, 453, 469; *a → o*, 379, 495; the final vowels, 436–437; personal pronouns and pronominal suffixes, 208, 212, 434, 438; the word כתנת, 455

Phone *y* 452

Phoneme 491–493

Phonematic significance 452, 457

Phonology 368, 375, 452–518

Piyyuṭ

various words and forms 48, 222, 240 334, 375, 441

Place of origin of the Scroll 89–95

Place names

~ and dialectical research, 67; ~ indicating the geographical distribution of final *mem/nun* interchange, 61; the gutturals in ~ 510; ~ in the vicinity of Jerusalem, 89, 94; מדין, 61; צוער, 69–71; בית צפור, רמון 201; גופנא, 91; סרת 453; חוקק 457; חלן 456; בצרה, צמר 454; צפורין, גת רמון 459; בית השטה 469; נקב, 486; צפר, 480; לד, שקמונה 479; כרתים, 492; כרמל, עספיה 498

Place names, see also different items in pp. 96–125

Plural

Aramaic forms, 207–208; the pron. suf. ־כי not found after ־ות, 211; the word

חורי, 235; ‎־ות instead of ‎־ים, 321;
double ~ 399; הררים etc., 372; abstract
noun indicating the ~ 370; פסילים ניעים
etc., 379; new ~ form of ארמון, 367
Poetry, 232; see also: Late poetry
Popular etymology 113, 187
Popular texts 74, 77–89, 308
Prayers
influence of the language of the ~ 37–
38, 225–226, 271, 313, 543; pausal forms,
334; the form השכל, 321
Prefix
~ taw in the third pl. masc. of the imperfect 325
Prepositions
~ influenced by Aramaic, 214; ~ re-
peated before a noun in apposition, 410;
emending asyndetic relative clause, 431;
substitution of ~ 44, 223, 263, 403–410
Present
general ~ 349, 350
Pronouns
personal ~ 49, 52, 208, 209, 433–440;
proleptic ~ 559, 560
Proper nouns 96–125
~ in יקטל pattern, 104; ~ with ‎־יהו
‎־יה, 104; final u in ~ 114, 120; abbreviation of ~ 121
Pronunciation
~ of resh, 531; ~ of the ‎־או,־וא spelling, 168–171; ~ of final daleth, 227,
517; ~ of the qutl pattern, 502–503;
various words and forms, 19, 51, 396,
499, 500, 508
Pronunciation traditions of the Jewish
communities, see: Communities
Prophetic perfect 355, 356
Protasis, see: Textual influence
Pshiṭṭa, see: Versions
Pun 251
Punic
plene spelling in the ~ inscription, 7;
u → i, 453; quttul and qittel patterns,
464; various words and forms, 52, 181,
212, 445

Qames
~ representing either a or o 247, 473–
474
Qere 519–521

Rabbinic Hebrew, see: Mishnaic Hebrew
Rashi 230, 243, 257, 278
Reading(s)
~ based upon a Midrash, 100; see also:
Superiority
References
linguistic ~ 12–13, 48, 58, 60N, 70, 75,
80–81, 91, 205, 225, 237, 253, 258, 294,
516
Relative clause
asyndetic ~ 44, 320, 349, 422, 424, 431–
432; congruence in ~ 430
Relative pronoun
זו, זה 232
Replacement
of archaic forms 193, 324–325
Resh
influence of ~ 480; pronunciation of ~
531; dissimilatory ~ 515; omission of
final ~ 237
Resh, see also: Labials and resh
Revision
~ in Symachus 309

Samaritan Hebrew
~ and Hebrew dialectical research, 67;
the Scroll and ~ 566–567; u → i (a),
54, 452, 453, 467, 469, 487, 493, 496;
pronunciation of צאן ראש etc., 168–170;
pronunciation of לא, 19; pronunciation
of the suffix ‎־יו, 51; the forms of the
imperfect and the imperative, 196, 337;
puʻal conjugation, 140; quttul pattern,
487; personal pronouns and pronominal
suffixes, 72, 435, 436, 446, 447, 449, waw
consecutive, 42, 351; the word כיתנת, 475

Samaritan Pentateuch
points of contact between the Scroll
and ~ 91N, 102, 314; Aramaic influence
on the ~ 25; the ~ a popular text. 73–
74, 85; spelling in the ~ 151, 158; yod
representing short i, 158; yod representing final e, 158–159; the spelling יא‎־ 180;
sin/samech interchange, 185; various
spellings, 21, 155, 168, 176, 177, 187, 381;
weakening of the gutturals, 510; the taw
of hithpaʻel, 345; afformative ‎־תי sec.
pers. fem. sing., 190; קטלה third pers.
fem. pl., 192; אקטלה form, 327; צוי,
הבדילתי (instead of צו, ותהי), 328; ותהיה

etc., 197; passive *qal*, 362; asyndetic relative clause, 431; collective nouns, 398; את in the ~ 413; ילידי, 379; חית – חיתו, 387; various words, 57, 97, 100, 102, 204, 215, 228, 251, 283, 288, 368, 384, 391, 453, 455, 462, 474

Scribes, see: Parts of the Scroll

Scroll
Rabbi Meir's Pentateuch, 52, 56, 87, 88, 500, 517; the *Torah* ~ of the Synagogue of Asverus (Severus), 57, 88–89, 162, 185, 251; a Bible ~ found in Jerusalem, 91; Dead Sea Scrolls, see: Word index

Seals
the form of the suf. ־יהו in ancient ~ 4, 123

Second Temple period
the language of the ~ 4, 5, 8, 50, 72, 104, 105, 123, 124, 173, 196–197N, 201, 226, 252, 268, 283, 327, 336, 337, 339, 340, 351, 378, 379, 400, 437, 439

Septuagint
method of the ~ 74–75; the philological tradition of the ~ 309; interpreting Biblical Hebrew according to Aramaic and Mishnaic Hebrew, 74–75

Septuagint, see also: Versions

Severus, see: Scroll

Shewa
the ~ not used as full vowel, 566–567; preceding an *aleph*, 56, 202; ~ in the transliterations, 119, 500–501N; ~ = following vowel, 475, 500–501; assimilating to the following vowel, 476; ~ = *a*, 501; ~ before *aleph*, *ayin*, *heh* = o, 498–500; ~ before *beth* and *resh* = o, 497–498

Siddur
still containing the suffix כָה, 48

Slow speech 499

Sound change
u → i, 53, 54, 65, 452–456; *u → y*, 491; *ā → ō*, 494–496; *a → o*, 247, 277, 278, 369, 381; near gutturals, 237; *'imāla*, 495, 496

Spelling(s)
development of the ~ 141; special exegetical and methodological notes about ~ 21, 22, 141–145, 142, 168, 171, 174, 180, 184, 186, 358, 434, 449, 476;

plene ~ in the Lachish letters, 7; ~ of the Nash papyrus, 129; ~ of the active participle of *qal*, 85, 127–129; ~ of medial *waw* and primary *yod* verbs, 126; passive participle, 129–130; infinitive absolute of *qal*, 130–131; ~ of verbal afformatives before pronominal suffixes, 131–132; ~ of the ending ־ין, 133; ~ of the plural suffix ־ות, 134; ~ of the יקטל pattern, 135–136; ~ of קטל pattern, 136–137; ~ of *qutl* pattern, 138–139, 503–504; ~ of *pu'al*, 139 ff. ~ of *hoph'al*, 145; *waw* for *ḥatef*, 147–148; consonantal *waw* indicated by double *waw*, 148; ~ of *hiph'il*, 149–150; *yod* as vowel letter, 148–159; ~ of the קֶל pattern, 151; ~ of the perfect afformatives and other verbal forms, 150–151; ~ of the masc. pl. suf., 153; ~ of the pron. suf., 155–156; *yod* designating short vowels, 156–158 362, 558; *yod* instead of *heh* as vowel letter, 158–159; ~ of consonantal *yod*, 159–160; *aleph* as medial vowel letter, 160–163; *heh* instead of *aleph*) as final vowel letter, 164; aleph in forms like קאם, 161; *aleph* as final vowel letter, 163–164, 284–285; ־וא,־או as medial vowel letters for *o*, 20, 21, 165–171, 389; ־וא,־או as medial vowel letter for *u*, 174; ־וא, או as final vowel letters, 171–175; ־אי,־יא as medial vowel letters, 175–178; ־יא as final vowel letters, 178–182; ־אי as final vowel letters, 182; ־וה as final vowel letters for *o*, 22, 182–184; ־ה as third pers. sing. pron. suf., 184; ־וה as final vowel letters for *u*, 184; ־יה as final vowel letters, 184; ־אה as final vowel letters, 185, 513; *samech/sin* interchange, 185; the ~ יו = ו, 447; defective ~ in various words, 279, 281, 321, 343, 369; היה = אהיה, 356; the ~ of the afformative תה, 440–442; defective ~ in pronouns and pron. suf., 446–447

Spoken Hebrew
glide in ~ 516; ~ in the Second Temple period 336, 337

Standard and substandard 46–48, 51, 54, 62–64, 66–68, 170N, 195, 202–203, 336–338, 340, 442, 447, 457, 481, 500

Status
   superior ~ of a language 29
Stress, see: Accentuation
Substitutions
   ~ of conjugations, 42–43; ~ of roots,
   216–315

Substitution of words, see: Text
Substratum
   Hebrew-Aramaic ~ in Arabic 493–494,
   496
Suffixes 45–51, 72, 115, 209–215, 392, 440–
   451; see also: Endings
Superiority
   ~ of the Scroll's reading 124 305, 311–
   312, 320, 321, 324, 386, 387, 399
Suspended letters and words 522–531
Syndetic constructions 442
Syriac, see: Aramaic
Systemzwang 467, 468

Targumim, see: Versions, Aramaic
Taw
   assimilation of ~ 345–346
Technical term 233, 269
Tel el-Amarna, see: El-Amarna letters
Tenses 41–42, 346–358, 394
Tetragrammaton 216, 218, 241
Text
   emendation of the Biblical ~ (by the
   Scribe), 17, 18, 30, 32–44, 73, 84 et al.;
   proposed emendations parallel to the
   Scroll ~ 231, 232, 235, 238, 239, 244,
   245, 248, 256, 257, 258, 261, 264, 265,
   267, 268 270, 273, 276, 277, 281, 284,
   286, 311, 317, 320, 322, 345, 348, 350,
   373, 374, 385, 393, 396, 398, 399, 407,
   445, 466; parallelism, 229, 231, 234, 237,
   238, 241, 249, 269, 270, 273, 384; para-
   phrase of the ancient ~ 73; simplifica-
   tion, 305; approach of the Scroll, the
   versions and the modern commentators
   to the Bible ~ 306–307, 311

Textual influence
   ~ of protasis, apodosis or of other Biblical verses on the Scroll version 289,
   291, 320, 323, 369, 395–397, 401, 404,
   406, 407, 408, 537–550, 552, 553, 554,
   558, 559, 561, 562
Textual harmonization 305, 307, 312, 321,
   348, 349, 350, 352, 355, 359, 361, 392,

395, 396, 397, 400
Textual conformity 75, 76, 219 220, 221,
   224, 227, 228, 229, 231, 234, 235, 236,
   239, 244, 250, 258, 263, 280, 288, 289,
   308, 312, 377, 386

Textual omissions 547–555
Torah scroll, see: Scroll
Transcriptions
   the pronunciation of the word ראש in
   Egyptian ~ 169
Translation
   double ~ 293
Translations, see: Versions

Transliterations (Greek and Roman)
   the ~ and the Scroll, 16–17; reflect-
   ing the substandard, 47, 62–63, 337–
   338; Aramaic forms, 77, 197; Mishnaic
   Hebrew influence on the ~ 457; dialectical variation in the ~ 62–63; ~ from
   Jerusalem, 94–95; influence of the labials
   and *resh*, 56, 497; the Tiberian *qameṣ* in
   Hieronimus' ~ 380; final *mem/nun* interchange, 61; the pronunciation of the
   shwa, 110, 498, 500–502; auxiliary vowel,
   337N; assimilation of *taw*, 346; *u → i*
   interchange, 461 469, 472,492; dissimilation of vowels, 53–54, 469; loss of voice in
   final position, 517; final vowels in the
   Septuagint, 437; pronunciation of the
   pers. pron. הוא, 436; pausal forms in
   the ~ 194–195, 335–337; the forms of
   the imperfect and the imperative, 342,
   470; verbs third guttural, 195; קֶטֶל →
   קוֹטֶל, 341; perfect afformatives and pronominal suffixes, 45, 49, 51, 64, 213, 440,
   442, 446, 447; the gentilic suffix, 515;
   qutl pattern, 55, 68, 461, 503, 504; the
   segolate patterns, 471; *waw* consecutive,
   45, 351; ~ of proper nouns, 96–125;
   Akkadian ~ 436
Transliterations, see also: Word index

Ugaritic
   the orthography of ~ 6; final vowels,
   436; locative *heh*, 414; preformative *taw* in
   third pers. pl. masc. imperfect, 325; personal pronouns, 434, 438; various words,
   33, 180, 181, 255, 293, 315, 366, 458, 460
Underlying text of the Scroll 85, 174, 243,
   289, 313, 378, 546

Var. lect.
  ∼ of Hebr. Mss. 314
Verbal noun
  להקטלוּת, 200; טבחה, 375
Vernacular texts, see: Popular texts
Versions
  agreeing with the Scroll, 35–37; defective spelling in the underlying texts of
  the ∼ 144; emendation of the ∼ in ac-
  cord with the Hebrew original, 309; rare
  Hebrew words in the ∼ 310; importance
  of the ∼ in understanding the Scroll,
  308, 309; var. lec. within the ∼ 309;
  philological tradition of the Septuagint,
  309; prepositions, 403–410; conjunctive
  waw, 414–429; misc., 19, 98, 216–315,
  325, 429–432, 536–564
Voice
  loss of ∼ in final position 517
Vorlage, see: Underlying text
Vowel(s)
  ∼ with two maxima, 170; auxiliary ∼

68, 337N, 502–504; dropping of the final
short ∼ 436–437; connective ∼ in proper names, 105–106
Vulgar texts, see: Popular texts

Waw
  ∼ conjunctive, 351, 357, 431–432;
  ∼ consecutive, 41–42, 351–355, 427, 428;
  ∼ incorrectly placed, 508, 509; ∼ of the
  apodosis, 354, 355, 422, 423, 427, 428;
  double ∼ representing consonantal ∼
  292; ∼ indicating *qameṣ* or *pataḥ*, 247,
  277, 278, 369, 381
Word(s)
  ∼ with two forms, 492; rare ∼ in the
  Scroll, 310; ∼ order, 430

Yemenite tradition
  the pronunciation of the *shewa* 501
Yemenite tradition, see also: Communities
Yod
  yod → *aleph* 511–516

INDICES OF WORDS

WORD INDEX OF 1QIsᵃ

— א —

יאבדו 165
יובדו 165
אובד 349
אובדים 127
תאבו 165
אביונים 396
אבילי 155
אבילים 6, 155
אבליו 155
אבלך 209
אבן• 309
אבניך 210
האבנים 216
אבניטך 155
אגודות 145
אגורי 511
אגמן 205, 365, 457
אונמן 205, 365, 387
גורף 202
ידומו 331, 341, 363, 505·
אדום 6, 137
האדמה 216
אדנות• 216, 218
אדס 57, 506
ואדרהה 150, 330, 345
אוהבי 127, 320
אוהבים לנוח 429, 499
אהבת 189
אהל 502
אהלכי 209, 210, 502
אוהל 502
אוהול (second ו sus-pended) 55, 502
או 220, 313
אובות (first ו sus-pended) 132
אודו 506

אוי 390
אולים 152
אולם 506
אוצרותי 134
אוצרותיו 132
אאור• 310
יאירו 32, 216
אור 132
אורות 134
אות 132
אותיות 217
אותות 217, 308, 397
לאות ולמופת 401
ויאזן 432
האזינה 6, 154
האזינו (ה suspended) 506, 507
האזיני 149
ואזינו 506
אחן 138
אזני 146
אחני 6, 143
אחנים 143, 145
אוחנכה 146
אחיהו 443
אחד 392, 517
אחז• 313, 314
יאחז (א suspended) 505
יאחז [?] 296
ויואחז (א suspended) 165
יאחזן 165, 193
מאחזי 217
אחרונה 365
אחרונות 365
אחרות 366
אוטם 128
איי 159, 512, 515
איים 512
אים 512

אים (י suspended) 153, 512, 514
מהאיבו (ה suspended) 128, 505
אייאמים 159, 161, 217, 309, 512
איך 389
איכה 389
היכה 389, 390, 505
אילי 390
איאל 160
אילים 152
אין 218, 307, 311
ואין מים 256, 311
איסו 172
אנשים 219, 305, 307, 312
אנשי מדות 398
אגורי 511
ואוכלה 128, 165, 326
[יאכולוהי =] יאכולוהו 165, 477
יאכולוהי 213, 331, 341
יאכולם 331, 477
יאכל 165, 400, 476
יאכלו 165, 476
יאכלם 165, 331
ייאכולם = [יואכולם (first י suspended)] 165, 331, 477
יואכל 20, 43, 165, 476
יואכלו (י suspended) 165, 476
תואכל 165
תואכלו 165
תאכלם 165
אוכל 127
אוכלת 127
אכול 130
אכולו 193, 347

אסיריו 366
אסרחדן 91, 96, 124
אסרחדן בניו 443
אפיא 179
אפו 172
אפוא 172
אפודות 397
ומאספלה 367
אסע 367, 507
אתאפקה 326
אצבעותיו 134
אצית 221, 507
אוקדה (ו suspended) 368, 478
ארא לם 36, 283
ארבות 146
יירגו 149, 331, 356, 505
ארואל 97, 98
ארזיך 221
ארח 138, 141, 143
אורחותיו 145
אורחותיך 145
ארחיבי 506
ארי 368
אריה 368
ויארך 330
האיריכי 185, 200, 516
אורך 209
ארמנותיה 367
ארמונתיה (first ו suspended) 367
אורן 138
ארץ 413, 508
ארצכמה 49
ארצמה 49
אררט see הוררט
אש 36, 221, 306, 307, 308
ואש 506
אשדודה 414
אשו 531
אשורה 414
וישמו 292, 505
אשמה 135, 326
אשמונים 368, 387
אשסא 163
•אשר 313
מאשריו 139
משריך 498, 499, 505

20 [יומר = יומר•]
ונאומרה 39, 165, 326
תאמר 165
תאמרו 165, 193
תואמר 165
תואמרו 165, 193, 395
תואמרי 165
תאומר 165
תומר 165
תומרו 165
האומר 349
אמורו 193
אמורי (י suspended) 193
לאמור 6, 136
אמורו נא 193
אמרי 478
אמריכמה 478
אמרים 127
אמרת 189, 478
אמרתי 188, 478
אמרתך 478
אנה 507, 506
אני 148, 179, 219
אניא 179
אניות 143, 149
אוניות 6, 143, 148
אנכי 219
אנוכי 133, 219, 314
אנוכיי (first י suspended) [?] 160
אנשים 219, 305, 307, 312
אנשי מדות 398
•אסף 306
אסף 138, 139
ואספה 220
אספו 139
כאסף 136
נאסף (א suspended) 57, 505
נספים 57, 505, 509
מאספוהי 213
[מאספיהו] = מאספוהי 443, 447
•אסר 313
אסור 366
אסורה 350, 361
ותאסר 220

כאכל 136
לאכול 348
ואוכלתי 200
הכן 502
אכס 218, 313
אל 404, 405, 507
ואל 404
אליו 430
אליך 405, 507
אליכמה 49
א־ל אלוקים 219
על 408, 409, 410, 506
אלה 218
אלים 144, 152
אלוקים 218
אלמן 457
אלמנה 38, 366, 508
באלמנתו 51
אלמנתיו 134
אלמנתיך 134, 210
אמלל 400
אמללה 191, 392
אמיניך 127, 210
תאמינו 154, 331
תיאמינו 185, 200, 243, 516
אמץ 152
•יאמר 313
אמר 127, 165, 219, 326, 353
אמרו 194
אמרה 393
ואמרה 165, 326, 327
אומר 165
ואומרה 39, 326, 357
ואומרה (second ו suspended) 165, 326
יאמר 165, 170, 365
•ריאמר 531
יאמרו 165
יואמר 20, 165, 168, 356, 360, 402, 476
יואמר (ו suspended) 165
ויואמר 357
יואמרו 165, 219, 398
יאומר 165, 168

הביאותיהו 342, 443
הביאותיו 131
הביאותים 131, 342
ויביא 149, 345
הביו 516, 519
להביא 41, 346
ואבוסה 326
בור 132
יבושו 126, 357, 358
בזאי 231
בזוי 347
יבזזו [ובזזו = ו] 344
יבחו 136
בחזינו 127
בזח 130
לבז 136
בחיניה 392, 519
•בחן 314
בחנתיכה 223
בחן 138, 143
בחר 130
בחרתמה 441
אבחר 341
אבחרהו 341
ויבחורו 331, 341, 357
יבחר 341
יבחרכה 341, 355, 432
בחור (ו suspended) 130
בטחו 41, 347
אבטח 326
בוטחים 127
•בין 313
נבותים 126
הבינותמה 131, 441
יבינו 223
בינות 399
בצי 6, 144, 152
בציהמה 144, 152
בצים 144, 152
בית בית 403
ביתה 414
הבית 414
בכו 173, 182
יבכא 163, 328
יבכיון 325
תבכו 398
ביכורה [?] 157, 476
בל 312, 313, 390
בלאדן 99

במה 444, 448
בבבל 406
בבורה 406
בבית נסרך 405, 410
בהר פרצים 406
בהתכנס 406
ובזבחיכה 405, 410
בחזק 405
בחרב 404, 410
בטמה 405
ביום אחד 405
בכיס 406
בכליהמה 405
בכרמי 406
בלוא שבעה 404
בלבבו 405
ובמגורותיהמה 406
במעברה 405
במעמקי ים 405
במרום ובקודש 406
בעיר 406
בעת 406
בצל 406
באשים 174
באושמה 148, 167
באש 222
לבב (לבבל) 122, 314
בבבל 414
יבגודו 331
בוגד 128
בגוד 130
לבדכה 156
בוהלה (ו suspended) [?] 477
בהמות 399
•בוא 305
בא 126, 223
באה 185
ובאה 392
באו 400
יבוא 403
ויבוא 430
יבואו 398
ותבואה 328
תבואינה 151, 342
בוא 21, 172, 173
בואי 126
בואי (ו suspended) 126
הביאותיה 131, 149, 342

יאושר 222
אשר 44, 431
את אלה 412
את אשר לוא סופר 412
את אשר לוא שמעו 412
את אשר עשו 412
את אשר שלחתיו 412
את בן רמליה 412
את בריתכמה 412
את גפנו 412
את ה' 412
את המשל 412
את הרע 412
את השמש 412
את חרבותם 44, 412
את ירושלים 412
את עבדו 412
את פניו (את suspended) 412
את פריאם 412
את שאר (את suspended) 412
את תנתו 412
אתכמה 444, 448
אותו 392
אותוה 22, [183]
אותם 405
יאתיו 325
האתיו 162, 188, 505
אתיו 222, 324, 325
ואתין 325, 348
אתה 222, 313, 507
אתי 208, 405
אתם 405
אתמה 49, 433 ff.

— ב —

באה 161, 444
בה 444
בהא 444, 451
בו 172, 173, 392
בוה 22, 183
בי 179
ביא 179
בכה 442, 446
בכי 209, 210

ריגדל 150, 330, 430
גדל 138, 141, 143
גודל 138, 141, 143
אנדע 326
גדעו 139
גודפים 53, 475
גדרי 227
גוי 148
גוך 148
גוי 512, 401
גואים 511, 513
גרים 512
גולת 370
[גו]לתיא 179, 370
יגר 356
גורלכה 209
גורף 202
[גזולי?] גזיל 155
למול 136
גזלת 155
יגזר 135
גי 180
גילה 326
גיר 152
גליתה 189, 209
תגלה 328
גלו 137
ויגל 328
גליון 133
מגוללה 142
גמא 138, 164, 508
גומא 164
גומה 138
גמול 133, 203
גמולות 133
גמאלם 20, 160, 567
גמותי 131
גנן 130
ריגער 357
גסן 201
גוסן 24, 201, 496
גר 151
גרשו 431
נשש 326
בגד 227, 517

– ד –

דאגת 189
דב 143

בראוש 22, 168, 177
ברוש 168
ברחו 194
ברחוה 183, 184
ברך 316
ולברך את שם ה' 37, 225, 313
בורך 24, 201, 477
בורכים 24, 201
בשם 143
בושת 138, 143
בשת 138, 143
בושתכמה 145
בת אחד 392
בתה 160

– ג –

גאה 369
גאתו 369
גאי 180, 226
גאוה 369
גאון 226, 369
גאות 134, 155, 226
גיאות 134, 155
גאלתי 344
גאלנו 127
גאלמה 49, 444
גאולים 130
•גואל 305, 312
גואלך 277
וגואלכה 209, 213
גואלכי 27, 209, 211
וגואליו 443
גבה 137
גבהים 146
כגובה 320
גבהות 134
גבלות 133
גבולותו 443
גבוליך 396
גבוריך (emended to גבורותיך) 370
גבורא 163
גבורת 370
גבורתי 132
גברתה 370
גוותיה 134
בגד 227, 517
גדותיו 207

בלוי עץ 224, 312
ובליה 224
בליו עץ 224
אבלע 326
מבלעים 139
במה 368
(א suspended) הבאמות 161, 368
בומתו 225
בומתי 368
במותיו 134, 368
בניו 51, 443
בנך 156
בן גדרי 227
•בנה 313
ויבנא 328
תבנינה 151
בוניך 225
(ו suspended) בוניכי 225
בסו 126
בסור 201
תבעון 39, 324
בעו 39, 324
כי כבעול 348, 406
בעלכי 209, 211
בערתמה 441
תבער 44, 431
בערה 127
בצי 6, 144, 152
בציהמה 144, 152
בצים 144, 152
לבצור 361
[ב]צורה 130
בצורות 129
בוצרה 6, 145
יבקעו 356
נבקענה 149
בקעה 478
בוקק 128
בוקר 6, 138, 141, 143
בקר 138, 141, 143
בקשוני 131
בראתיהו 443
ויברא 357
בורא 128, 164
(י suspended) בוראיכה 154, 156, 396
בורה 164

דבור 371
דבר (participle) 127
דברו 347
וידבר 128, 349
דבר 227
הדגים 38, 370
דודנים 100
דוה 371
דוות 228, 313
דויד 5, 99
ידיקנו 362
דורות 133
תדוש 209, 213
[הדש = הדוש] 505
כחדוש 57, 506
ידש 363
דיבון 101, 102
מדוכא 139
מדכאים 139
דלתות 388
תדמין 325
תדמיוני 76, 312, 325
•דממה 310, 312
דממה 371
מדממתך 134, 228
•דעת 307, 312
בדעתך 209, 228
ידיקנו 362
תדק 135
יודק (ו suspended) 364
ידרוך 135
דרוכות 129
דרכוהי 192, 213
דרכי 397
דרכיך 396, 400
דרמשק 3
ידרוש 135
ידרושו 331
דרשו 194
דרושו 193
דשא 164
דשה 164
ידשן 139

– ה –

ה־ (definite article) 411
הה, הא־ 444, 447

האזורה 20, 161, 162
חוברי 233, 506, 520
והגה 229, 313
הגורה 507
הדום 133
הדוש 505
אדס 57, 506
הדר 130
הדריכה 349
חחים 235, 506
הו־ 443, 447
הוא 433, 565
הואה 52, 433 ff., 564, 565
הוה 183, 229, 306, 433
הויה 229
הורט 56, 102, 124, 497, 505, 566
הי־ 24, 64, 213, 214
היא 163, 433, 565
היאה 52, 433 ff., 565
היה (= היא) 184, 185
היה 159, 352, 354, 356
היהא 42, 185, 354
היהא (א suspended) 185
היו 353, 354, 397, 398, 399
הייא 159, 163
הייה 159
היית 159, 343
הייתה 159
הייתמה 441
אהיא 163
אהיה 356, 507
ויהי 329, 353, 357
ויהי (first י suspended) 357
יהיה 42, 57, 159, 329, 357, 358, 401, 507
יהיה (first י suspended) 353, 357
ויהיא (first י suspended) 357
ויהיה 357

ויהיו 357, 399
ונהיה 329
תהיה 42, 329, 355
תהיו 159
ותהי־ [?] 158
ותהיי (second י suspended) 329
תהינה 151, 329, 342, 508, 566
היותה 159
הייותך 159
ויהיה בער 403, 409
היכה 389, 390, 505
הכרות 24, 200
•הלך 312
הלכו 355, 397
אלך 326
אלכה 326
וילכו 357
תלכו 193, 229
תלכון 193
נלכה 326
נאלכה 20, 162, 187, 326
הולך (ו suspended) 127, 128
הולוך (first ו suspended, second ו erased) 348
הלוך 130, 348
להלוך 346
ואהלכו 507
התהלכתי (תה suspended) 364
והוליכתי 154, 197
תלב 250
•הלל 306, 307
ויהללו 357
והוללו 230
אולם 506
הם 433
ההם 507
להם 445
המה 49, 392 433, 434, 438
להמה 397, 445
המה־ 49, 445, 449
יהמין 325
עמסים 57, 506

חובשו 139
חוגה 145, 163
הגורה 507
חגורו 193, 348
חגרנה 342
כחדש 57, 506
חדלו 194
•חדש 143
חודש 138
חודשיכם 145, 146
חוד[שו] 146
•חול 305
[ת]חולין 193, 234
יחילון 193
התחיל 177, 364, 393
חומות 38, 388
חומותיך 134, 210, 211
חוצות 132
חוצותיה 134, 392
•חור 309, 310, 311
חורו 234, 235
יחורו 148
יחיש 328
חזית 189
חזה 127
חיים 235, 506
יחזיק 325
תחזיק 325
חזון 206
חזות 134
חחיר 374, 387
חזיין 206
חזקו 194
והחזיקה (ח suspended) 27, 57, 191, 192, 506, 507
ואחזיקה 326, 345
לאחזיק 506
בחחק 373
חזקת 478
חזקיה 4, 103, 104 ff., 565
חחקיה 4, 55, 103, 477, 565
חזקיה המלך 429
חוטא 6, 164
חוטה 127, 164
חטאו 374
חטאי 399
חטאת 374

•זד 306, 311
זדיך 210, 231
זה 232, 308, 310
•זוב 312
הזיב 233
האזורה 20, 161, 162
נזרו 126
זכרת 189
זכרתי 188
יזכור 363
תזכורי 40, 330
נזכור 363
תזכרו 401
יזכרוכה 331
זכור 136
זכרו 193
זכורנא 136
הזכירוני 398, 399
אזכיר 363
יזכירו 363
מזכירים 149
זכרונכה 209
זכריה 4, 103
זמרת 134, 135, 152
ותזגו 398
זונה (ו suspended) 128
הזניחו 345
•זעק 34, 314
זעקו 233
זעקך 209
זקנה 478
מזוקקים 6, 139, 140, 142
יזרה 356
זרעו 133
זורע 127
זרעו 133, 140, 194
זרעך 209
זרעכה 156
זרעם 133

— ח —

הוחבאו 145
יחבוט 135
חבל 139
חוברי 233, 506, 520
חובריו 373
חובריך 372

הן 214
אנה 57, 506
הנה 214
להנה 445
־הנה 445, 451
הנומה 445, 450, 496
הסך מכם 316
הרבות (ה suspended) 57, 506, 507, 509
הרג 130, 140
אהרוג 326
הורגיו 350
הרוגים 130
תהרגנה 566
הרוה 182, 184
הרסך 352, 443
הרוסתך 209, 372
מהורסיך 56, 210, 473, 496
הריסתך 134
הררים 231, 372
השקי 507

— ו —

ו־ 414–429
־ו 51, 443, 447
־והי 24, 64, 213, 214
־ות 207
וקטלת 191

— ז —

זאב 499
זב 56, 498, 499
בזאי 231
זאת 20
זאות 20, 167, 168
זואת 20, 167, 168, 394
זואת (א suspended) 167
זות 20, 167
זותה [זות emended from זה ?] 233, 306
זבול 133
זבולון 132

חורב 138
חורבה 143, 144, 146
חרבות 146
חרבו[ת]יה 146
חרבותיה 146
חרבותיך 143, 146
וחרדו 395, 398
החרדים 340
החורד 340
חריהמה 505, 520
חורי 147
החרס 506
אחריש 34, 239
והחרישו 354
חרש 138, 238
חרשים 239
•חורש 308
חורש 473
חורשי האדמה 238
חורשי צורים 76, 238, 313
חשבנוהו 131
חשבנוהי 131, 213
יחשוב 401
חושב 239, 350
•חשה 239
אחשתי 506
חשוכה 24, 203
חשוכים 203
[חשוכים=]חשיכים 155
תחשוכי 330
חושך 138, 142
חשופי 130, 193
לחסוף 136, 185
השקי 507
וחשש 506
חששה 240, 307, 375
חותו 136
החתת 344

– ט –

לטבוח 316, 348
טבח 316, 375
לטבחה 243, 375
טוב 240, 308
היטיב 154
טמיתם 505
טמא 164
טמה 164
טרח 141
טרסיו 443

יחמולו 331
יחמולו (first ו sus-
pended) 331,
403
חומלתיו 443, 477
חמותי 131
ויחום 145
לחומם 374
חמים 237
חמר 138, 144, 505
חומר 375, 496
חמשא 163
מת 108, 506
יחון 402
חנן 130
יחוננו 145
חוננו 145
חנף 138
ובחסדי 399
חסדיו 443
חסות 134
חסן 138
לחסוף 136, 185
חפזון 133
יחמצון 193
ותחפורו 330
תחפורי 330, 341, 363
חפור 363, 506, 507
לחפרפרים 389
פשיים [ח] 512
חצבתם [=חצבתמה]142
חצבתמה 139, 441
חצבי 127
חצה 133
חציר 238
חוצן 138
חצר 33, 237
חוק 137
חוקה [= חיקוה] 8
חוקותיך 213, 321
חוקקי 127, 375, 387,
478
יחרוב 341
חרוב 131
אחריב 326
אחריבה 326
ואחריבה 326
חרביא 21, 179
הרבות (ה suspended)
57, 506, 507, 509

חטאתיכה 134, 167
חטאותיה 167
חטאותיך 374
חטאותיכה 167
חטאותיכמה 167
חטאותינו 167
חטאותמה 167
חטר 138, 143
•חיה 306, 308
יחיה 235, 507
ויחיה 235
ותחיה 329
לחיות 39, 345, 506
חיו רוחו 316
חית 38
חיות 387
חיזקיה [=חזקיה] 157
חילם 399
חיקוה 22, 183, 184
חכמתך 209
חל 152
חלית 189
חולי 6, 147
חוליו 145
בחוליותי 146, 321, 347
חולייו (second י sus-
pended) 148,
154, 512
•חלל 306
ואחללה 325
ויחללהו 326
מחללה 394
מחללת 126
יחלומו 331, 399
לחלף 136
יחליצו 394
תחליץ 359
חלצי 130, 144
חלק 139
חלקכה 189, 209
חלקיה 103
•יחם 313
כחם 137, 237, 531
נחמדנו 443
חמדה 375
חמתיא 179
חמת אסוא 429
•יחמל 310
יחמול (ו suspended)
34, 237

— י —

יאור 167
יארי 167
יאים- 38, 39, 511–513
יבור 57, 507
יברכיה 4, 103
•יבש 311
יבש 136, 149, 353
תיבש 241, 505
וייבשו 149
אוביש 326
יגעת 189
יגעתי 188
יגע 149
יגעו 149
ייגעו 149
ידוהי 213
ידיך 155, 401
ידיכה 401
ידיו נטויה 51, 443, 447
יודכה 126
תודכה 126
אודו 506
ידומו 331, 341, 363, 505
ידעו 348
ידעכה 401
ידעתי 188
ידעתיא 179
ידענו 128
ואדעה 326, 507
ונדע 326, 507
נדעה 326
נודע 393, 507
יודע 350
אודיע 326, 507
והודיע 453
יודיע 126, 241
יודינו 516
ָיָה (-יָהוּ) 4, 122, 123
יהה, יהא- 444, 447
יהו- 443, 447
ין- 51, 443, 448
יודינו 516
ביום (ו suspended) 132
יומי (ו suspended) 24, 204
יואן 160

יונא 163
•יחד 309
תחת 265, 517
יחד 390, 391
יחדו 241, 390, 391
יחדיו 390, 391
יחזקיה 4, 104 ff., 565
יחזקיה 4, 104, 565
יחזקיה (first י suspended) 104, 565
יחזקיהו 4, 104, 105
אחל 242
יחלו 361
יוחילון 193, 361
היטיב 154
ים- 38, 39, 511–513
יך- 442, 443, 446
יכה- 442, 443, 446
יכל- 307, 310, 313
יכלו 399
יוכיל 242
יוכלו 355
ילדת 127
ילודי 376
ילד 139
והולידו 347, 522
יהליל 198
ייליל 198
אילילו 506
הילילו 506
תילילו 198
יליל 198
ים-• 38, 39, 511–513
יימן 306, 309
תיאמינו 185, 200, 243, 516
ין- 207
ינקתי 189
מינקותיך 150, 210
וינקו ידים 243
יסדו 396
יסד 127
יתוסד [= תוסד י suspended] 156
מיסד 350
ליסד 136

יסודותיך (תיך suspended) 210, 322
•יוסף 220
נוספת 134
ויוסף 150, 156
תוסיף 126
תיסיף (first י [?] suspended) 201
ויסרהו 443
יעודה 130
יעיל 272
•יעף 308, 309
יעיף 154, 243
יעף 149, 155, 243
יעפו 149
יופיו 6, 146
יעץ 128
יועץ 128
יעקוב (ע suspended) 57, 137, 507
יעקוב 6, 137
•יער 305, 312
היער 76, 244, 508
יערו 274
יצא 127
יצאה 191, 192
הוציאו 348, 399
הוציתי 505
יצע 145
אצק 135
יצר 135, 349, 401
יצרה 127
יצרתיהו 443
אצורנה 147, 331
ויצורי 331
יוצרו 127
יוצריו 443
ויוצריכה (second י suspended) 156, 390
יקד 136
אוקר 150, 326
יקשון 193
•ירא 310
ייראו 149
ירא 163, 284
ויראו 149
יראי 397
תיראו 244, 506
•ירד 312

כילי 152	כמדבר 407	ירד 127, 245, 354
כימן 157, 474	כמכה 407	לרדת (ת suspended) 39, 344
כל 137, 141, 143, 147	כמצות 406	ואורידה 326
כול 6, 137, 141, 142, 143	כמשק גבים 403	יוריד 245
כולם 6, 445	כרוב עצתך 407	ירא- 163, 284
כולמה (ו suspended) 146	כאוב 376	מורה 126
כולמה 444	[כאוב = כאיב] 155, 175, 499	מולֹך 253
•כלה 311	נכאי 182, 265	ירוק 202, 376
כלה 183	כבד 32, 138	ירושלים 5, 106, 414
כלו 248	כבדו 191	ירושלם 5, 106
יכלה 248	כבדים 246	•יירע 310
יכלוון (ו [?] sus- pended) 324	ואכבדה 39, 326	וירעו 246
ככלותך 32, 131, 248	מכבד 140	יירשו 398
כלה באש 183	הכבדתי 188	ירשוה 149
כלאיות 160, 501	תכובה 139, 358	[ירשוהי =]393
כלמות 157	כבוד 202, 246, 314	וירשוהי 214
•כמה 312	•כבוש 314	ירש 128, 149, 400
כמה- (כם-) 49, 444, 448, 564	כבושים 247, 308, 473	•יש 313
•כנה 313	כברים 32, 152	תשב 364
יכנפו 396	כובס 128	יושב 128
כסא 164	כה- (ך) 45 f., 64, 442, 443, 446, 564	יושבי 128, 399
כסה 164	כה 183, 184	יושבי (ו suspended) 127
יכסו 364	כוה 8, 22, 183, 184	יושבת 226
תכסך 213	כוהן 127, 322	ישומון 54, 474, 476
ויתכס 328	תכוה 148	ישועות 134
כסותם 134	•כן 307, 308, 310, 313	והושיעו 43, 360
כפיכמה 451	הכינכה (י suspended) 247, 505, 509	הושעתנו 316
כפר 43, 140, 362, 402	להוכין 39, 345	הושעמה 444
יכפר 139	יוכן 356	אושיענו 506
תכפר 139	תתכונני 345	יושיעוך 131, 149, 213
לכפרה 346	תכוני 189	יושעכמה 49
כופרך 6, 146	כוח 137	תושעון 193
כרובים 133	כוחה 22, 183, 184	ישעיה 4, 107
כריתות 134	כי 178, 180, 247, 307	ישעיהו 4, 107
כורכובות 249, 309, 496	כיא 8, 21, 178, 181, 248	ישעיהו (ע suspended) 507
ואכרות 326	כיא (י suspended) 178, 180	וישתם 246, 364, 441
ואכרותה 40, 326, 330	כיי [?] 160	וישתם בדכם 403
תכרותו 400	כי אעלה 178	יתדותו 443
ותכרותי 189, 209, 330	כילו (י suspended) 171, 178, 250	יאתום 20, 160, 567
לכרות 136	כימי 178	יותר 148
להכרית 345	כי- (ך) 27, 64, 209, 210, 211	
כשדיים 38, 512		— כ —
יכשולו 331, 360		כאסס 406, 407
כשול 130		כבין חציר 407
		כבעול 407
		כחזקת 409

כתוב 130, 136
כותבהא (ו suspended) 194, 196, 431, 444, 478
כתים 512
•כתנת 6, 145
כתנו[תיך] 399, 475
יוכת 6, 145

– ל –

להם 445
להמה 397, 408, 445
להמה (מ emended to נ) 392
להנה 445
לי 179
ליא 21, 179
ליאאתה (first א suspended) 171, 179
לך 209, 210, 442, 443
לכה 210, 442, 443, 446
לכי 27, 209, 211
לכם 395, 448
לכמה 249, 444, 448
לארצו 408
לגוי 408
לדברי 408
ולמצא 407, 410
למצרים 407, 410
למשוסה 407
למשפח 407
לעדרים 407
לצדיק 407
לרצץ על מזבחי 408, 430
לשלום 407
לתהו 407
לתהו ולהבל 407, 410
לו 172
לוא 8, 20, 21, 171, 174, 249, 305
בלוא 171
הלוא 171
ללוא 171
לואאדם (first א suspended) 171

לוא הגדלת 171
ולוא חלה 432
ולוא ידעו 44, 432
לוא יודע 349, 431
ולוא תדעי 432
לוא תוכלי 432
ולוא ילדה 432
לוא ייליל 172
ולוא תועיל 348
ולוא מות 431
לוא שותה 349, 430
לכן 171, 250, 307, 312
לאוט 390, 474, 477
לאות ולמופת 401
לאומי (ו suspended) 146
לאומים 6, 146
לאחזיק 506
לאשקיט 57, 346, 506
•לב 313
לב 204
לבב 314
לבבך 204
ובלבב 204
לבכה 189
לבכי 209, 210
לבדכה 156
לביא 178
ילביגו 149
לבש 130
אלבישה 326
להב 377
להבה 377
להבי 377
להבים 377
לוהבת 377
לוה 127
נלוא 163
הנלוים 512, 515
•לוח 309
לוחות 107, 115
לוחיי (second י suspended) 250
בלחם 387
לוחצים 127
תותלוצצו (first ו suspended) 127
לחש 316
לחשו 316

מליל 377
בלילה 377
ליליות 397
ילין 149
ליץ 151
ליש 107
ילכודה 331
לכן 171, 250, 307, 312
למדי 475
למדו 194
מלמדה 139
למודי 475
למודים 475
למו 449
לנואם 22, 56, 171, 177, 499
לנסה 345, 506
לעת תזכור 511, 517
ליץ 151
אקחה 395
היקחו 364, 402
נקח 357, 395
ילקח 43, 364
לוקח 139
תלקטו 139
לקראת 160
לקרת 160, 505
לשונמה 49

– מ –

‑ם 49, 444, 445', 448, 564, 565
מאדה 499
מאוד 167
מאדה 251, 413, 414, 498, 499, 565
מאד 56, 167, 498, 499, 565
מאדה 52, 498, 565
מאורות צמעונים 399
מחנים 24, 187
מזנים 24, 186, 566
מאכלת 138, 143
מאס 127, 128, 130
ימאסן 193
מאוס 130
•מאסכה 251, 314

מלאו 173
ומלו 343, 498, 505
ימלא 42
ימלה 164
תמלאה 42, 185, 355
מלאי 349
מלאים 340
נמלא 42, 352
•מלאך 311
מלאך 505
מלאיך 257
מלכי 209, 258, 505
מלוא 172
מלואה 167
מלואו (ו suspended) 133, 167
מלונה 132
ואמלטה 326
•מלך 305, 312, 531
ימלוך 135
המלך חזקיה 429
ממלכות 134
ממלכת 134
ממלכתו 258
מכמה 444
ממך 209
מנו 214
ממני 28, 214
מני 214
מן בנות 214
מן הוא 253
מן תאנה 214
מאשור משבט 511
מיין 408, 410
ממחסה 408
מעברת 408
מעשות 408, 410
משבט 408, 511
משלכת 408
נמנא 163
מנחות 134
מנוס 258, 306
מנוסא 163
מנחל 264, 506
מסולל 317
מסך 258, 313, 314
מסכה 259
מסכות 397
מסכן 139
מסכסכה 378

מוריך 253
•מוש 305
ימוש 254
•מות 308
ימותון 193
תמות 137
תמותון 126, 193
מית 151, 566
מיתי 151, 257, 311
מיתיך 151
מיתים 6, 151
יומת 403
המות 131, 254
מזבחותיו 134
מזח 254, 307, 310
מזנים 24, 186, 566
מחבה 164
מחגרת 138, 143
ממחים 140
מחמדינו 378
•מחץ 312, 315
המוחצת 33, 255, 315
מהשוכים 203, 205, 397, 507
מחשך 206
מטו 443
•מטל 314
למטלים 255, 312, 515
מטמוני 133
מטעני 140, 144
מי 178, 180, 312
מיא 8, 21, 178, 180, 181
ולמי 256
מידבה 108, 164
מיחים 157
מיים [?] 159
מי ים 256, 311
מי לחץ 429
•מיש 305
מות מית etc. see
מוכמר 117
מוכמר (ו suspended) 145, 478, 496
[מיכמר = מוכמר (ו suspended)] 157
מכמרת 138, 143
מכסך 154
נמכרתמה 441
מלא 172, 392

כמאסכת 251, 506
•מבטח 305, 306
מבטחם 252
•מגד 310, 312
ותמגדנו 252
ממגדסותם (second מ suspended) 377
מדברה 414
מדורתה 132
מדים 61, 108, 518
מדין 108
מה- 49, 444, 445, 448, 564, 565
מה[ו]א (?) 253
מהול 130
מהניף (ה suspended) 24, 198
מהסיר 24, 72, 198, 199
•מאסכה 251, 314
כמאסכת 251, 506
כמסאכת (א suspended) 57, 251, 506
מהר 152
מהשוכים 203, 205, 397, 507
מתלות 506
במו 449
מודד 253
מודד במודעיו 511
מודעות 399
במודעיו 253, 508
מודעים 153
תתמוטינה 151, 359
מוטה 153
מוסרותיכם 388
מוסריך 399
מועדיכם 132
מועדינו 155
מפת 132
מץ 132
המוץ 132, 230, 310, 311, 312
מור 378, 474, 477, 496
•מורא 305
מוראו 132
מוראיך 253, 505
מוראכם 132
מורה 126

÷ מקף 257 +

נואם 56, 167, 174, 498, 508, 565	מקרקר קדשו 118	מסלה 57, 157
מנאציך 210, 508	ומר 261	מסלות 157
מנאץ 139	מרבץ 378	מסלת 157
נבאות 109, 566	ימרו 39, 317	מסלתי 134
הבטחמה 441	למרות 345	כמסס 136
ואביטה 326	מרהבה 261	מעברת 134
הביטו 352	ממורט (ו suspended) 39, 140, 344	מעחו 146
נבי 21, 178		מעוזיה 146
נביא 178	ממרט 344	מעוזך 209, 398
הנביא 204, 515, 516	מרכבותיו 134	מעונה 139
יבול 135	המשרה 261	ממעיכה 259, 507
יבולו 331	המשרה (ו suspended) 261	•מעים 312
ונבולה 262, 326		מעינים 389
נבל 127	•משח 313	מעיף 317
נובל 347	משחתי 262	מעלה 403
נובלת 127	משכי 127	ממעלה 391
•ינבלה 308	ממשך 139	מעלליההמה 49
נבלתך 262	משכבותיו 401	מעשהו 154
וינידה 444	משכבכה 189, 209	מעשוהי 213
וינידו 399, 432	משכבמה 451	[מעשיהו = מעשוהי] 154, 213, 443
ינידונא 164	משוכתו 146	
ינד 145	משל 127	מעשיהו (י suspended) 154
הוגד 6, 145	משלה 127	
היגד 150, 156	משלו 127	מעשי 159
•נגד 309, 312	ימשלו 331	מעשקה 139
נגד 263	ימשל 135	כמפאכת (א suspended) 57, 251, 506
לנגד 263	תמשלוני (corrected from תמשולוני) 149	
נוגה 138		•מפלה 531
נוגה (ו suspended) 138	משלי 127	מצוא 172
	משלח 139	ימצאו 402
ננותי 151	משלכת 319, 511	והנמצא 266
תגע 263	משמה 413, 414	נמציתי 505
ייע 355	משוסה 55, 146, 363	תמצא 393
נוגע 477	[משסה = משוסה] 157	מצא 163
[מגיעי = מגיעי] 296	משריך 498, 499, 505	מצית 189
נגף 130, 347, 358	משתריים 159, 289, 506, 507	מצודות 132, 260, 312
ינש 341		מצת 189, 441, 505
יונשו 331, 341	מת 108, 506	מצתכה 134
נגשו 51, 127, 443	מית etc. see מות	מצער (ז suspended above the צ) 260
תגנשו 331	מתני 146	
נדד 400	מתנים 143	תמוצו 137
אדודה 263, 326, 330		מצרים 414
מנדח 139	— נ —	וממצרים 214
מדח 145		ומצרתה 132, 260
נודף 39, 344, 360	נאו 160	מקדשיו (י suspended) 443
[נידף = נודף] 156	נאולו 344, 498	
נדש 126	נאלכה 20, 162, 187, 326	מקניך 154
נהג 127	נאום 56, 167, 174, 499, 565	מקצעות 133
ינהל 264		מקראה 156

יצילוך 131, 213	נטש 139	ינחלם 264, 506
הצל 154	נכאי 182, 265	מנחל 264, 506
ואצורכה 145	הכהו 131	נהליולים (ו suspended) 379
נצרה 127	הכיתיך 213	נהרות 388
נצורות 129	יאכה 160	נהרותיך 522
נצורים 266, 311	ויך 328	נהרי 388
ובנצירים 380	מככה 209	נהרים 388
יקובנו 147, 331	תכו 145	נו- 443, 447
נקיא 178, 182	מוכה 6, 145	נוגע 477
ואנקם [= זואנקמה] 326	נוכחה 326	התנודדא 163
נקף 138, 478	נוכחה (ו suspended) 476, 478, 500	הנחתמה 441
נק[ם]ה 478	נכוחה 476	יניחוהי 131, 213
נקרתם [= נקרתמה] 142	נכוחות 476	נוי צואן 159
נקרתמה 139, 441	נכחות 476	לנואם 22, 56, 171, 177, 499
ישייכה 516	הכירנו 352	תנוסון 193
נשא• 311	נכריאים 38, 512	ינועו 126
נשא 127, 130, 163, 172	נכריה 512	נוע (ו suspended) 126
ישא 403	נכתיו 183, 443	ינוף 361
ישאוהי 131, 213	ונס 401	מהניף (ה suspended) 24, 198
ישאון 193	לנסך 136	מניפיו 443
תישאום 6, 156	נסוכה 130	לנפה 345, 506
תשאני 267	נסך 258	ויזל 400
שא 163	נסכי 379	נחל• 307, 309, 310
סאי 185	נסכהמה (י suspended) 379, 387	ינחילו 265
נושא 127	נסס 127	ינחלם 264, 506
נושא (ו suspended) 163	נע 126	מנחל 264, 506
נושאים 350	ונע 109, 506	אנחם 326
נשוא 172	נעליך 399	ינחמך 213
נשא פנים 144	נעמונים 379	תנחמו 144
ונשאו 402	מנעציך 508	תתנחמו 362
הנשא 505	נער 127, 128	מנחם 349
תנשנה 151, 505	נעורת 138	נחמה 140
תנשינה 393, 505	נעשף (ע suspended) 507, 509	נחושת 138
ישיגו 193	לנסה 345, 506	נטא 163
נשיא• 310	נפל 136, 392	ויט 328
נשיאי 266	נפלה 393	יטי 312
אשומה 330	יסול 135	נוטה 128
נעשף (ע suspended) 274, 507, 509	יפולו 331, 397	נטוות 519
נתיבה• 305, 312	יפלו 331	נטיה 130
נתיבות 267, 389	מנפצות 139	נטיה (ו suspended) 130, 144
נתן 352	נשסוה 22, 183, 184	הטא 163
ונתנו 402	נסשותינו 398	ייטול [= וייטול] 6, 156
אתן 326, 355	נפשי 179	נטוע 194, 347, 508
אתנה 326	נפשיא 179	נטפות 144, 152
ויתנו 41, 347, 403	נפשיו 51, 443	
	נפשכי 209, 210	
	הצילו 352	

אתן האדם (the ה is suspended between the two words) 326
נתעם 296. 305, 313, 508
תתוצו 40, 330
ונתרת 191

– ס –

סאי 185
סאן 127
וסבאים 398
נסבה 185, 395, 498, 508
יסֹוב 363, 364
יסבלוהי 131, 213, 331
•סבל 143
סבלו 143
יסגוד 135
ויסגודו 331
סגר 139, 144
סגרו 139
סוגר 127
סודם 109 ff., 475, 476, 500, 504
נסגו 126
נסגותי 126
אסיג 506
•סח 5
סונים 111, 512
כסוס 522
ספות 132
הסיר 149
הסירו 149
הסירותי 268
יסירנו 268
אסיר 326, 346, 506
תסירו 348, 359
מהסיר 24, 72, 198, 199
הסיר פנים 314
סחורה 57, 507
סחר 127
סוכה 146
סלה 112, 507
סולו 6, 137
לסלוח 136

יסכל 185
•סמך 305, 313
סמכתו 443
נסמך 268
סנחריב 113
סרחריב 113, 124, 511
ולסעדה 392
סעסיה 152
סער 269
סחורה 57, 507
ספרתי 269
ספר 127, 128
סופר 139
הספר (ה suspended) 520
ספריים 112, 159
יסקולהו 331, 361
סקלו 193
•סרה 313
סורה 269
וסרה 223, 350
סרחריב 113, 124, 511
סרפוד 380, 474
סוררים 269
אהסתר 198, 346
מסתיר 149, 345
לסתר 149, 345

– ע –

יעבדו 358
יעבדוכי 27, 213, 331
עבדי 194 270
עבדו 402
לעבד 136
עבדתו 133
עבודת 132
עבר 400
יעבור 135
יעברו 331
יבור 57, 507
יועברנו (first ו suspended)
[יעוברנה =] 331
יעבורנו (first ו suspended)
[יעוברנה =] 340
יעברנו 331

נעבורה 330
עבורו 193
עֲבורי 193
עוברי 194, 478, 500, 501
עברי 194
עיברו (י suspended) 194
עוגר 317
עדקה 270, 313
יעדרון 193
והעד 348, 505
עד 151
עדי 391
עדי (י suspended) 391
עדים 151, 270
עוד 391
עודנה 270, 271, 313
•עוה 313
נעוו 37, 271
נעירתי 271
עאון 161
עוון 132, 161
עוונה 132
עוונתינו 389
עוונות 132, 134
עוונכה 132, 401
עויל 205
עול 137
עולך 146, 209
עולה 205, 271, 473
עולות 381
עולותיהמה 451
עוללות 134
עוללת 134, 135
עועיים 512
ויעוף 145
יעושו 272
תעופסנה 358
מעיף 317
העירותיהו 150
ויעיר 43, 357, 361
עואר 162, 163, 204
עור 162, 204
עורים 162, 163, 204
עוה 137
עוחו 146
עוחי 146
עזב 139

עניים 382, 399, 512
עניים [= עניים se-cond י sus-pended] 159
ענה 127
עוסל 138
עצב 143
עצה 155
עצתך 401
עצם 127, 128
עצמותיכמה (ה suspended) 134
עוצמה 6, 146
ואעצורה 330, 357
עצרתה 24, 205
עקב 137, 144
התערבונא 395
ערבי 401
ערות 508
עריץ 273, 311
ויערוכהה 331, 444
תערוכו 330
ערוך 130
[ויערוכהה =] ויעריכהה 359
לערוץ 136
יעריצו 149
מערצכם 149
עורערו 114, 497
עורסרה 451
עור[ר]ה 296, 392
עשה• 305
עשיתה 274
עשיתיהו 443
עשיתים 445
ויעש 328
ויעשה 328, 356
ישה 57, 328, 507
עשיה 127
עושוהי 213
[עושׂהי =] עושיהו 154, 443
עושהו 154
עושיך 210
עושכי 209, 210
לעשות 131
עשיריה 512
העושׂנים 340
עושק 138
עושקה 196

ויעלה 328
תעלי 189, 209
תעלינא 163
עלות[ו] 131
תתעל 273
העליתה 189
עלוחה 205
עלוחי 205
עלז• 305
ותעלח 35, 273, 507
עליזה 205
עליזי 205
עלילותיו 134
אעלים 149
עולסו 139
עמוא 8, 21, 172, 179, 181
עמו 172
עמי 179, 181
עמיא 179, 181
ועם עשיר 409
עם עבדיך 409
יעמדו 331
ונעמודה 330
עמד 127
ועמודו 353
עמודינא 193
לעמוד 136
עומרה 113, 475, 476, 500
עומסים 350
עמסים 57, 506
עמק• 312
והעמקים 273
ענוגה 146
ענונו 202
עונג 138
עננא 175, 191, 395
אענכה 355
ויעני 158, 328
תעננהו 131
ענים 382
עניים (second י sus-pended) 382
עני 178, 382
עניא 178
עניה 382, 512
עניו 151, 382
לעניי 382
עניה 157, 159, 512

ועזבו 353
עזבתיך 213
אעזובם 331
תעזוב 360
תעזובו 330
עוזבי 127
עזובות 129, 399
עוחז 53, 475
עחז 475, 500, 501
עוזיה 4, 113
יעזר• 309, 313
עזרתיכה 209, 213
אעזורכה 355
יעזור 135
יעזורו 331
יעזרו 331
ועזרכה 349, 432
עזר 130, 144
עזרי 272
לעזרה 381
עטה 182
עוטך [= יעוטך] 127
מעטרה 363
העכיסים 381
עיה 115
עיל• 313
עילוליהמה 381
בעיים 159
עיני 152
עיניכה 155
עינים 152
בעיניהם (ע suspended) 507
עיף 155, 243
עיסה 155, 243
עיסו 115
עיר 566
עיר החרס 5, 116
עיר מואב 116, 117
עירים 296
על 408, 409, 506
ועל פרי בטן 44, 408, 410
על תבינו 408, 410
על תדעו 408
עלוהי 24, 213, 408, 506
עליה 393
עליו 409, 506
עלית 189
עליתי 25, 188

194 עושקה לי
382 בעתה
517 לעת
511, 517 לעת תזכור
507 אתה
506 עתה
432 ועתה תצמח

– פ –

213 פארך
475 פגולים
150, 362 יפגע
134 סדות
184 פה
179 פי
179 פיא
444 פיה
443 פיהו
126 נפוצות
274 ופזורי
353, 395, 398 ופחדו
326 אפחד
393 תפחד
164 פלא
164 פלה
164 להפלה
164, 343 הפלה
343 הפלה ופלה
275 תפלט
275, 511 'יהפליט
152, 163 פליטא
152 פליטת
515 פלטיש
134 פלצות
38, 512 פלשתיים
512 פלשתים
130 פסח
451 פסלמה
367 אפעה
39, 330, 341 אפעולה
341 יפעל
341 יפעלהו
55, 502 פועול
502 פועל
146, 502 פועלכה
146, 502 פועלכמה
502 פעלכם
383 פעל
383, 502 פעלת

57, 498, 508, 509 פועלתי
498 כועלתמה
443, 499 פעלתיו
499 פעולתכם
6, 135 אפקוד
135, 363 יפקוד
136 לפקוד
146 פקודה
146, 322 פקודותי
146, 209 פקודתך
308 'יפרה
127 פריה
275 ואפרהו
130 פרח
276, 357 ויפרח
(ו suspended) 498 פורי
161 פריאם
403 פרי מעלה
130 פרוס
183, 184 פרעה
22, 183, 184 פרעוה
130 פרע
330 תפרוצי
154 הפירו
403 פרש
40, 331, 395, 444 יפרושה
127 פרשי
194 פשטה
326 אפשעה
127 פושעים
347, 508 פשועי
383, 396 ולפשעיהמה
155 פשעינו
154, 401, 508, 509 פשעכה
פושעתים [?] (ו suspend-ed) 512
445 פתהן
137 פתאום
137 פתאם
352 פתח
353 ופתח
276, 347 פתחו
191 פתחת
326 אפתחה
122, 506 תפתח
127 פותח

191, 392, 507, 509 נפתחה

– צ –

144 צאה
20, 166, 168 צאן
168 צאן
20, 166, 168 צואן
צואונו (first ו suspended, second ו erased) 166, 167, 508
166 צואנכמה
הצאצאים (first א suspended) 505
496 צוב[י]ם
172 צבא
127 צבאים
127 צביה
152, 383 צדק
209, 210 צדקכי
6, 148 צהורים
161, 188 צואר
161, 188 צורך
276 תצוו
516 תיצוו
148 צום
158, 328 צורי
308, 310, 312 •צוח
277, 473, 474 צוחות
305, 306 •צור
132, 277, 278, 566, 473, 474 צור
132, 272 צורים
512 ציים
207, 278, 306, 310, 512 ציין
278 צי לצי
185, 512, 513 ציאה
512 ציה
278 ציון
306, 307, 308 •ציר
279 צירי
279, 306 צל צל
191, 192 הצליחה
164 צמא
164 צמה
133 צמאון

קרא• 310
קרא 32, 127. 164, 172, 394, 508
וקרא 354
וקראו 42, 173, 402
קראוהי 194, 213
קראת 393
קראתה 392
קראתי 34, 160, 283, 313, 505
קרתי 160, 505
קרתיהו 443
קרתיכה 160, 505
יקרא 164, 402
ויקרא 432
יקראו 44, 360, 402
ויקראם 395
יקרה 164
תקרוא 174, 360
תקראו 395
תקראון 193, 325, 326, 343
לקרוא 346
קורא 128, 164
קורה 164
קראים 127
קרוא 172
מקראי 140
קראתכי 213
קרבו 348
נקרבה 326, 341
תקרב 341
תקרבה 328, 341
אקרב 341
קרב 341
קרובו 39, 193, 194, 341
קרובה 323
קרס 127
הקשב 150
היקשב [= הקשב] 156
יקשב 149
אקשיבו 506
קשרים 475
קשתותיו 134
ובקשתות 43, 397

– ר –

ראה• 284, 306, 307, 311

יקומון 173
קומנה 137
הקימותי 131
הקימה 392
קור 118
יקשון 193
קטלתי 25
קטלתה 440
קטלה 27
קטלתמה 441
אקטול 39
אקטלה 39, 40, 326 ff.
יקטול 341, 342
יקטולו etc. 40, 41, 330 ff.
יקטולון 193
נקטלה 326 ff.
קטולי, קטולו 27, 191 ff.
קוטל 340, 341
לקטיל 345
קוטול, קטול, קוטל 55, 68 ff., 109 ff., 201 ff.
קטן 144
קיה 184
יקולל 139
קמוש 475
לקנות 131
קוניהו (י suspended) 154, 443
קסמים 127
קוסד 281, 282, 475, 476
קסוד 281, 282, 476
קפז 281, 282, 312
וקפצו 353
קץ 283, 314, 566
קצי 282
קצה• 313, 384
מקצהו 384
קצאות 160, 207, 567
קצוות 160, 207
קצוי 384
וקציר 323
אקצופה 330
יתקצף 358
קצרא 163
קצרו 318
יקצור 135
קצור 130
קצרו 193

יצמחו 358
יצנפכה [= וצנפכה] 331, 358, 442
צניף [= צנוף] (י suspended)] 130, 322
צניף (י suspended) 322
צועה 508
צעה 279
צען 138
צעור 69
צופה 127, 347
צפעה 144
צפעות 152
צפעונים 399
צפורים 6, 147
צצחות 506
צר 132, 279, 306
מצריי [= מצריו] 159
צרה 279, 305
יצרח• 312
יצריחו 37, 280

– ק –

קובעת 146
קובציך 53, 475
אקבצך 213
יקבצו 348
מקבצו 443
קוברך 56, 496
קדים 281, 311
קדמותה 383
קדקד 144
קדרות 134
יקדשו 150
התקדישו 154, 331, 347, 353
והקדישו 43, 149
קדש 138, 141
קדשו 146, 281
קדשי 146
קודש 138, 141, 146, 383
קודשי 146
קודשנו 146
ויקו 328
נקוה 431
קוי 127, 148
יקומו 126

ראיתה 347
ראיתמה 441
ראו 173, 352
ראוו 518
אראה 284, 355
ירא 163, 284
יראה 355
נראנו 443
תראה 285, 355
תראו 398
תראינה 151
ותראיני 189
ארא לם 36, 283
ראה 127
ראינו (ו[זו] suspended) 127, 154
מראות 131, 166
בראותו 131, 166
הראה 97, 284
הראיתים 445
ראמים 155, 499
ראוש 20, 22, 166, 168, 170
ראוש (ו suspended) 166
ראושה 166
ראושו 166
ראושם 166
ראש 20, 166
ראשיכם 166
רואש 8, 20, 166, 168. 170
רואש (ו suspended) 166
רואשו 166
רואשיהמה 166
בראשיו 51, 166, 443, 447
רוש 20, 22, 166, 168
ראישון 20, 171
ראישונה 175
ראישונות 175
ראישון 20, 175
ריאשן 22
ריאשונים 175, 474
רישן 20, 22, 172, 175, 474
רישונה 175

רישונות 175
ראשית 175
רוב 6, 137
רבא 163
ותרבי 189
הרבו 353
מרובה 139, 140, 318
רבץ 378
ירבוצו (second ו [=י] suspended) 331, 363
ירביצו (י suspended) 149
ירבק 285
רגזה 392
הרגזה 345, 346
ארגיז 326
רוגזך 146
רגליהנה 49, 445
רגליו 443
ירגיעו 355, 397
רוגע 477
יתרגשו 359
ורדים 127, 349
ירדופו 331
וירדפם 331
רודפי 127
מרדף 145
רדף 139
נרהב 57, 507
רוביך (emended from ריבך) 396
רוחחו 156, 443
רוח בוא 430
•ירום 310
מתרומם 345
הרים 230, 307. 312
הרימותה 131
אריס 132, 326
ירים 286, 239, 359
רום 132
•ירוע 307
הריעו 241, 286
יריעו 241
נרהב 57, 507
הרחבת 189, 209
ארחיבי 506
רחב 138, 143, 478
רחבת 478

רחוב 287, 306, 308, 506
רחוק 323
רחוקה 287
מרחק 133
•ירחם על 44
ירחמו 44
רחמתיך 213
מרחמכי 209, 210
ירחק 209
ירוטש 6
ירוטשו 139
ריבו 149
רוביך = [ריביך (י suspended)] 210, 384
לריב ולמצא 407, 410
•ירים 311
ריקה נפשיו 443, 447
רוכב 127, 318
רוכב (ו suspended) 318
רככה 139
רוכסים 208
[רומליהו = רומליה] 4, 118, 497
רמליה 4, 118, 497
וירמוס 135, 432
לרמוס 41, 346
רונה 54, 157, 323, 458, 474, 476, 477
[רונה = רינה] 157
ירונו 6, 137, 286
ירננו 42, 344, 348, 358, 402
רונו 137, 145
רעיהו (י suspended) 154
ירע 393, 507, 509
תרעינה 151
רועה 127
רועים (ו suspended) 127
רעי 127
רעותה 134
ירועע 139
ורסתיהו 160, 443, 505
ותרסו 172, 343, 347, 358

נרצא 163
רצין 118
רציאן 5, 118, 119, 161
רוקחיך 53, 210, 475
רוקע 127
רתקות 133, 144

– ש –

שאבתמה 49, 441
שאה 126, 127
שאול 133
שאון 323
אשאל 326
אשאלם 432
שאנות 505
שאנות (א suspended) 505
שאנכה (א suspended) 505
ואשופה 326, 330, 341, 505
שארית 385, 499
[ושריתו = ושירתו] 498, 505
שריתו 56, 498
שבאו 120
שבויים 153
שבט 401
שבי 497
שבישים 152, 185
שבל 205
שבלת 143
שבלים 475
שובנא 56, 496
שובנא (ו suspended) 120, 121, 496
שבנא 120, 496
שבע• 313
הנשבע 289
שבעה 143
[ש]בעין 207
לשבעת 429
שבעתמה 441
שברו 403
אשבור 326, 360
ישבור 135
לשבור 136
שבורו 193

שברן 385, 387
בשבתה 394
שגשנש• 313
תשגשנישי (first י suspended) 154, 287, 331
שד 137
ושדד 353
ישדד (י suspended) 353
שודד 139, 142
שדה 384
שדי כובס 159
שדף• 307, 308, 309, 313
הנשדף 289
שא 163
שו 21, 392
שוא 174
שבתה 296
וישוב 137, 145, 290
ישובו 193
ותשוב 145
ישב 137
שובו 126
שובי (ו suspended) 56, 497, 498
והשיב 353, 505
השיבותיכה 131
ואשיבה 149, 326
אשוא 163
לשאוות 290, 506
שוט 132
שט 319.
שולח 52, 121, 475/6
ותשרי 126, 189
שוחד 502
שוחוד 55, 72, 502
שחוד 502
שחה• 305
שוחי 477
והשתחו 291
והשתחוו 291
ישתחו 291
ישתחרי 158
ישתחוה 291
ישתחוו 291
ישתחוה 148, 291
יהשתחוו [ז] 199
תשתחוו 291

להשתחות 291
משתחוה 291
ישח 355
שוחי 477
השח 294
השחה (second ה suspended) 507
שחט 130
שעיס 507
שחר 152
תשחיתוהי 213
להשחיתה 348
משחיתים 149
שט 319
ישטסו 331
ישטסוך 331
שוטף 128
שוטסים 127
שיבה 385
שים• 305
שמת 189
שמתה 189
שמתי 188
ושמתיהו 44, 394
שמתיך 213
שמתיכה 213
אשים 326, 355
אשימה 326
וישם 156
נשימה 326
תשימוני 131
תשימי 451
[משימו =] משימי 288
לשום 288
אשירה 326
ישיר 402
שירות 152
שיש 401
אשית 326
אשיתחו 506
השת 294
ישכובו 39, 331, 341
תשכבו 193, 341
שוכבו 139, 473
שכחתי 25, 188
אשכחכי 213
תשכחי 393
השכחים 340
מהשכל 150, 321
שכוליך 475

תשפוט 32, 293
שופט 128
שופטיך 127
שפוטונה 164, 193
שפכתה 189
שפלת 189
תשפולי 330, 341, 363
תשפל 76
תשפלנה 355
אשפיל 321
[ותשפולי = ותשפילי] 189
שפותי 293
ישפיקו 149
שקוץ 386
[אשקיטה = אשקוטה] 147, 326, 330
לאשקיט 57, 346, 506
•ישקל 313
שקל 127, 128
ישקולו 331
תשקולו 330
ובשקלו 293
שקק 128
שרי[כ]י 209, 210
שר אוצר 5, 119, 124
[שר אוצר = שראיצר] 155
•ישרה 313
שרופות 129
ישרוק 6, 135
ישרו 137
ישריש 149, 345
שורש 138
שורשיו 147, 208
שורשך 146, 209
שרש 138
שרשו 140, 394
שרשם 143, 146
ישרתונך 213
•שת 313
שת 126
שתה 182
שתו 182
שתיתי 189
[ישתוהי = ישתוהו] 443
שותה 349
שותיו 127
לשתותו 44, 394

השם 292, 344
•שמע 393, 400, 401
שמעה 194, 328, 507
שמעו 164, 194, 348
שמעוא 172, 175, 508
שמעתי 189, 191
שמעתמה 441
ואשמע 326
ישמעו 348, 399
ונשמעה 293
שומע 6, 127
שמעי 194
שמעי נא 194
שמוע 130, 136
לשמוע 136, 346
אשמיע 326
ישמיעו 359
השמיעו 394
השמיעונו 131
לשמיע 345, 506
משמיעיהמה 292
ישמרו 331
שמרו 193
ושומרים 396
שונה 164
כשני 398
שנונים 130
שוסינו 154
שועו 500, 501
תשענה 151, 508
שעיס 507
שועלו 146
שעפי 151
שער 413
השערה 414
וישעשע 42, 357
תשעשעו 144
התשעתשעו (second ת suspended) 346
תשעתשעו 362
השע 344
שעשועו 443
שעותי 293
שמאותיכה 167, 168, 177, 389
שפאים 511
•שפט 293
ישפוט 135
ישפוטו 331
נשפטה 326

ישכונו 331
ישכנו 331
שכן 127
שוכן 340
ישכורו 331
ישכרו 193
שכורת 129
אשכירמה 361
שכרון 324
שולח 52, 121, 475, 476
שלומים 475
שלומכה 156
שלוש 132
שלושה 132
שלח 136, 354
אשלח 326
ותשלחי 189
שלוח 341
שולחה 139
שולחן 146
שוליו 132
שוליך 32, 291
•שולים 310, 312
שליש 152
ישליך 149
יושלכו 145
הושלכתה 145
שלמה 288, 305, 313
משלם 139
ישלים 149
שמיא 179
שם 413
משמה 413, 414
שמה 292, 413
שמאול 167
שמואל 167
להשמיד 149, 345
שמועתו 324
ונשמח 326, 507
שמחי 340
משמט 296
שמים 404, 410
שימיר [?] 385
שמלה 288
שמלתנו 288
שממה 386
ושממו 319
וישמו 292, 505
שוממה 386

תומך 295
תומם 146
כהתממך 257
תנים 296, 306
תנחומים 38, 386
מתעבי 399
תועה 127, 349
תועי (ו suspended) 127
•תעם 305, 313
תפים 141
תפראת 57, 508, 509
יתפוש 135
ויתפושם 40, 331
כתקוע 6, 136
תרהר 294, 313
תרן 138
תורתן 51, 122, 496
תשאות 132
תתמוטינה 151, 359
תתעל 273

תחלתי 506
תהרהר 294
תו 172, 174
תועבה 132
לתועבות 398
•תורה 313
תורות 134
תורתך 163, 295
תחלתי 506
מתחת 413
מתחתה 413, 414
תחות 24, 214
תחת 265, 517
תי- 25, 188 ff.
תלב 250
תלבושת 138
תם 137, 401
תומם 146
תמה-, תם- 49, 441
•תמך 305
תמך 136
אתמוכה 39, 330

שתות 131
נשתע 293
שותתיה 205

— ת —

ת- 440, 441, 446
•תאיה 313
תאית 294
תנתו 56, 498, 505, 509
תאור 202
תוארו 146, 202
תבונתיו 443
תבלותם 386
תה- 45 ff., 64, 440, 441, 446, 564
תהוו 203, 516
תומות 498, 506
תהי 294, 313, 329
תהלת 134, 157
תהלתו 157

WORD INDEX OF THE THANKSGIVING PSALMS (1QH)

כלות 131
לא 173
לוא 173
להוב 203, 377
תלכוד 136
לצים 151
מגבל 140
מדהבה 261
מחסי 159
מי 181
מכמרת 139
וימס 154
למיס [= למוס] 154
מקוי 159
משאה 127
משואה 127
משקלת 139
מותני 147
נגיעים 379
הוגשתי 145
ידיחני 132
הניסותה 131, 342
[נ]כאי רוח 265

חוליים 148
חומץ 139
חמר 139
חוקים 147
חקוק 130
יחשבוני 132
יחשוב 136
[אתחשב = אחשב] 136
[?] החתתה 131
[?] טאטאיי 160
ידעים 128
יצר חמר 505
יושר אמתכה (first ו suspended) 502, 503
[כאוב = כאיב] 154
[נ]כאי רוח 265
הכינותה 342
כי 180
כיא 180
כל 137
כולם 147

אוני 147
אוניה 148
האירותה 342
תאוכל 166
אף הוא 440
אפהו 440
אפהוא 440
אורך ימים 503
ארוך אפים 203, 503
הביאותה 131, 342
לבחון 136
בנים 152
גדול 203
גזעו 157
גזעם 157
גיזעו 157
ותגל 157
[זהויות = הווות] 148
היותם 131
זכרון 133
מזוקק 140
חבתה 151

לשת [= לָשֵׁת] 149	לסתוח 136	יתגשגו 287, 346
נתיבת 135	צודוק [= צירוק]	ותשב 157
סבבוני 132	157, 476	ותשימני 149
תסמוך 136	צידוק [= צירוק]	ותשמני 149
סופר 140	157	לשת [= לָשֵׁת] 149
תסתירני 150	קודשו 147	שוחד 503
לעבדך [= ולעובדך]	ראשון 176	וישומעוני 337
147	ראשונים 176	לשפוך 136
לעובדך 147	רב 137	שרירות 134
להעיז 154	רוב 137	שרשיו 148
עון 132	רבי 152	תהו 203
עיני 152	ריבי 152	(?) (תה]יל[ה] 157
עצה 155	רנה 157	אתמוכה 332
ערמה 147	שאה 127	תרן 139
הפלתה 151	שבה [= שיבה	
פתאו[ם] 157	(י suspended)]	
מפותי 140	152	
פיתאום [= פותאים]	שיבה 152	
157	ישוברו 140	

WORD INDEX OF THE GENESIS APOCRYPHON

דברת 152	סודום 504	ראישה 177
חולק 148	סודם 504	רגג 152
ירתעי 152	עולימא 148	מרים 199
כל 137	סורת 91	שבאו 173
מגן 199	קודם 148	ישכח 199

WORD INDEX OF THE MANUAL OF DISCIPLINE (1QS)

לאהוב 136	לדבוק 136	טמאה 147
הנשי 509	בדעהא 185	יומי 24, 204
יואכל 166	ידורשהו 336	וכירשתו 147
יואכלו 166	ידרושהו 132	ישור לבבי 203, 502, 503
יוכל 166	לדרוש 136	נכאה רגלים 265
אומר 166	הווא 163	כבוד אוזן 203, 502, 503
אמר 166	נהייה 159	כובוד לב 55, 203, 502, 503
יומרו 166	להלכת 199	
אפיא 181	הנשי 509	יהכין 198
אסהואה 440	זואת 167	כל (inflected) 147
אסוא 173	זות 167	כי 180
הובדל 145	חודשים 148	כיא 180
מובדל 145	חטתו 161	ניכנעים [= נוכנעים] 157
להבי 180	חושך 139	תכופר 140
יהבינהו [ז] 198, 199	טהרה 147	אכשיל 360
להברך 346	טוהרה (first ה sus-	לוא 173
גבורתום 474	pended) 147	

137 רב	132 יסקודהו	204 לב
137 רוב	146 סקודת	204 לבב
135 ארדף	280 יפתח צרתי	515 לויים
203 רחוב נפש	280 ובהפתח צרה	449 למו
136 לרחוק	173 לקרוא	140 מגבל
137 רוע	132 יקרבהו	206 מחשך
131 לרצת	139 קודש	379 נעים
132 ישלחהו	148 קודשים	135 אטור
167 שמאול	203, 503 קוצר אפים	265 נכאה רגלים
173 לשנא	203, 503 קצור אפים	150 אסתר
341 [ישפל =] ישפול	164 קורה	132, 150 יסתרהו
203 שפול ידים	139 קושי	150 לסתר
134 שרירות	139 קשי	135 יעבר
139 שורש	167 ראש	509 נ[ע]ונעש
214 תוחת	167 רואש	147 ערמתו
137 תום	167 רשו	146 סעולתם
136 תתם	144, 152, 176 רשונה	135 יסקוד

WORD INDEX OF THE ORDER OF THE WAR BETWEEN THE CHILDREN OF LIGHT AND THE CHILDREN OF DARKNESS (1QM)

128 עשה	377 לוהב	166 תואכל
134 סדות	140 מלומדי	132 יביאום
151 הפלתה	140 ממחזים	128 בחרים
515 פלשתיים	159 מחני	144, 152 ביניים
184 פרעוה	181 מיא	144, 155 בנים
91 פורת	154 [מוס[לר] =] [מיס[לה]	136 תבצור
140 מפותחים	154 להמס	139, 144 גדל
131, 342 הקימותה	531 (suspend-ed ער) מערכת	139, 144, 147 גודלו
147 קורבם	531 (suspended ר) מערכת	151 תהיינה
167 ראש	159 מעשי	131 היות
167 ראש	143 מותני	131 הלוך
176 ראישון	143, 147 מתנים	133 זכרון
176 ראישונה	265 נכאי רוח	147 חודשיהם
140 מרודד	136 בנפול	131 לחנות
136 לרדוף	531 [corrected from סרוכים] סדורים	137 חוק
136 לרדף	185 ססות	147 טהרה
136 ברדף	185 הסרים	147 טמאה
147 רוחבו	136 יעמוד	160 ידי
147 [רוחבו=] רחבו	332 יעמודו	160 יידי
139 רמח	147 בעומדם	130 יעוד
139 רמחיהם	203 עצום ידינו	149 תיראו
157 רנות	332, 333 יעורכוה	265 נכאי רוח
131 הרעונו	147 עורסם	128 כוהן
157, 477 רוקמה	159 עושי	180 כיא
157, 477 ריקמה		133 כידן
147 שולחן		137, 147 כל
167 שמאול		332 יכתובו
531 (suspended ר) שמרתה		515 כתיים
		173 לוא

תום 137	הסרים 185	ספות 185
תומה 147	תהו 203	לשפוך 136

WORD INDEX OF PESHER HABAKKUK (1QpH)

עיצה (י suspended) 155	כשדאים 515	אמה 152
עצה 155	כתיאים 515	יאמינו 175
עורלת 146	לוא 173	יאמינא 21, 175
ערמתו 147	לאומים 147	ברי 180
עושה התורה 159	לדה 155	בשת 138
פיא 181	מאס 185	גופרית 146
הפלה 164	מאשו 185	דומה 371
למשור 136	מס[י]כה 155	הפלה 164
פתאי 513	משל 137	להרוג 136
קיצי [?] 151	יסופר 140	ולהרותם 127
קצוות 208	לעובדם 147	יחמל 136
קצות 208	יעבר 136	ינעו 149
רב 137	148 [בעוון=] ב[א]וון	הודיעו 150
רעיהו 154	עון 132	הודעו 150
רעיהו (י suspended) 154	עזרוהו 131	היים 160
שיו [=שוו] 21, 148, 174	עינים (first י suspended) 152	ייעפו 149
שומעם 147	על פרי בטן לוא ירחמו 408	ולהרותם 127
ישופטנו 336	יעלנו 151	ירושלם 106
	עומדו 147	יושרה 140
	לענותו 131	כי 180
	עושלה 140	כיא 180
		כל 147
		לכלות 131

WORD INDEX OF 1QIs[b]

בלאדן 99	ירושלם 107	נכאה 265
דויד 99	ישעיהו 107	עגור עגיר 317
לטבוח 316	מדין 108	עיפה 115
י[חז]קיהו 104	נביות 109	תרהר 294

WORD INDEX OF OTHER DSS

יאירו 286	הלחית 107	לוא 173
מאחרי 217	יומים 204	נבי 179
בוא 173	ירושלים 107	עיתה 115
בגדי רוקמ[ות] 477	ירושלם 106, 107	עתהא 185
דויד 99	כורים 497	שוקמים 459
דיבון 101	כתים 515	

WORD INDEX OF GREEK AND LATIN TRANSLITERATIONS

אביהוא 436
אבינעם Αβεινεεμ 458
Αβινοεμ 458
אבירם Αβ(ε)ιρών 61
אגמון agmon 206
אדמים adamim 463
אהבו αβου 195
אהליאב Ελιαβος 461
אחינעם Αχινας 461
Αχιμαν 461
איים ιιμ 218
איש his 509
אשה hissa 509
אלי Ηλει 182
אליהוא 436
אלם Ελλημος 471
אמצים amasim 463
אמרת εμαραθ 471
אסרחדן 96
אסעה ephee 368
אצם Ασαμος 461
אקדח ecda 368, 478
אראלם arellam 283
ארבע arbee 368
אריאל 97, 98
אריה aria 63
arie 63
ουριαν 284
αριηλ 284
ארצה Ολσα 461
ארט 101
בטחו βετου 195
בית זית Βεζαθα 89
בית פעור Βαιθφογωρ 110
בכי βεχι 459
בלאדן 99
בלע Βολος 461
בעז Βοωζης 504
Βοαζος 504
Βοες 504
Βοος 55, 504
בעל beel 64
baal 64
בצרה Βοσορρα 114
Βοσορα 114
בקבוק bocboc 456, 457
βακβουκ 456
בקבוקיה βακβακιας 456

ברדים borodim 463
בריח bari 315
ברכבעל Burucbal 454
Biricbal 454
בשור Βοσορ 110
בשר bosor 380
גב gab 63, 497
gob 63, 497
גדעון Γαδεων 469
גיורא γιωρας 77
גלגלת Γολγοθα 89, 455
גמר Γομαρος 504
גפנא Γοφνα 24
דאג δωηκ 517
דדנים 100
דיות dajoth 228
דימון 101
דמשק Δαμασκός 3
הוא hy 454
תהיו θου 329
לכו λχου 195
הם 435
הנע 109
יובלני jesbuleni
[= iezbuleni] 336
זכריהו 103
זמר Σιμυρα 454
חבה οβα 482
חדלו hedalu 194, 195
חזקיהו 104–106, 471
חלד ολδ 461
חלון Χαλον 456
χειλων 456
χελων 456
חלקיהו Ελκιαου 77
חלקיהו 103
חמץ Εμεσα 480
חמת 108
חנכת οννεχαθ 468, 500
חסצי ωφση 341
חקוק Ικωκ 457
Ιακωκ 457
Ιακακ 457
Ακωκ 457
חקל דמא Ακελδαμα 89
ויחרגו ουιερογου 335
חשבן Εσσεβων 105
יאשיהו Ιωσιαου 77

יד ιωτα 495
ידעו jadau 335
יה־ 123
ירדן Ιορδανης 56, 497
ישימון Ιεσσαιμου 474
ישעי ιεσσι 471
ιεσει 471
ישעך ιεσαχα 471
ישעיהו Ησαιας 76
־כ 501
כבוד Χαβωθ 517
כדכד χοδχοδ 456
chodchod 456
כי χι 180
chi 180
כל chyl 454
כמן κύμινον 453, 475
cuminum 453, 475
כסנתא Χαφεναθα 89
כרתים chorethim 56, 498
כתן (כתנת) Χιτών 53, 453,
486, 487
κιθών 453
Χεθων 453, 469,
486, 487
Χεθων 486
לב 204
לבש־ λαφσι 195
הלוחית 107
לחם λοομ 342, 500
לישה 107
מדין Μαδιάμ 61, 108
מדיני Μαδιανή 61
מהרה μηηρα 71
ובמשב ουβομωσαβ 498
אמחצם εμωστημ 335
מי μι 181
מלך Μολοχ 55, 503,
504
מנחם Μαναημ 502
מנשה Μανασση 502
ממעל לו memmallo 391
מצדה Μασαδα 260
מצלות mesuloth 463
משך Μοσοχ 462
(ה)משרה αμμισρα 261
misra 261
מתן Μεττηνος 454

	Μυττυνος 454
	Metun 454
	Mytthum 454
	Ματτην 454
	Muttine 454
מתקה	Ματεκκα 458
נאם	νουμ 500
נביות	109
נגה	Ναγεην 461
נכֹתה	νεχωθα 184
	nechota 184
נעמה	Νοομα 461
	Νοεμα 461
	Naama 461
נעמי	Ναανις 461
נעמן	380
יסלו	ιεφφολου 335
נצרת	115
(ה)נקב	Αννεκεβ 486
	Αννεκβ 486
	Νακεβ 486
	Ναβωκ 486
סדום	Σοδομα etc. 109 ff., 504
כסוס	Χισους 501
סינים	111
סלע	112
סנחריב	113
סרפד	sarphod 380
הסתרת	εσθερθα 197
עגור	αγουρ 318
	agor 318
	ακουρ 318
	αγρου 318
עזיהו	113
עיסה	116
עיר מואב	116, 117
עית	115
עלוהי	αλαυι 64
עממים	αμιμιμ 372
עמורה	113
עמרי	Αμαρινος 461
ענתה	anata 335
עֶזרה	Εφραν 461
עצרתה	ασαρθα 10, 205
עקש	Εκκης 471
ערוער	114

סגוּל	φεγουλ 469
פֶלג	φαλεκ 517
פלשתים	φυλιστιειμ 515
	Philisthiim 515
פסחא	πασχα 77
פרעוש	φορος 456
פרת	Φορας 91
פתחו	φθοου 195
אתפתח	εφφαθα 276, 346
צֹחַר	Σααρος 461
	Σοαρος 461, 504
ציון	Σιων 278
	sion 279
צלצל	selsel 279
צמר	Σιμμυρα 454
צֹעַר	Σηγωρ 69, 71
	Σιγωρ 70
	segor 70
	Ζογορα 69
	Ζοοπα 69, 70, 71
	Ζωωρ 69
	Ζοαρα 69, 71
	Zoarae 69
	Ζογερα 70
צפורין	Σετπφωρις 469
קֹטל	461
קֶטֶל	461
קֵטֶל	461
יקטולו	40
קְטֶלָה	Κοτολλα 501
	Catulla 501
קיר	118
קמוד	κιμμοδ 282
קראו	κερου 195
קראתי	carathi 190
קרסלי	χορσελαι 63, 457
ראש	ρος 169
	ros 169
	Ραως 169
	Αρος 169
	ρωσσος 169
ראש אדיר	Rusadir 169
רב	rob 497
רבי	Ραββι 65
	ribbi 66
	ριββ, ριβι etc. 65
רב יודה	Ραβ Ιουδα 65

רב יוסף	PIB ΙΩΑCΑ[Φ]65
רבקה	Ρεβεκκα 105, 114
רחוב	Ρωωβ 110, 501
רמליהו	118
רעו	dou 501
רעות	rooth 501
רצין	119
רן	ραννη 458
רנה	ρεννα 458
	ρενα 458
רֹתֶם	ραθεμ 458
רתמה	ραθαμα 458
שבא	120
שבנא	120
ישבר	ισουβερ 497
שבתא	10
משוה	μοσαυε 498
אשחקם	εσωκημ 335
שילוח	Σιλωαμ 53, 94, 95, 121
שלום	Σαλων 91
שלחי	Σαλει 459
שמאבר	Συμοβορος 461
שמעו	semu 195
	σιμου 195
שמעון	Συμεων 469, 470
	Συμων 469
	Συμον 469
	Σιμων 470
	Σεμεων 470
שפתי	σφωθαι 389
שקמה	συκαμινος 459
שקמונה	Συκαμινος 459, 472
שראצר	119
תלמי	Θολμαιος 461
תנים	thannim 63
	thennim 63
תעי	Θαινος 461
תֹפֶל	Τοφολ 458
תֹפֶת	θοφοθ 504
	θοφεθ 504
	θαφεθ 122, 504
	ταφεθ 504
תפתה	θαφθ 504
	θαφεθ 504
תרתן	122

LISTS OF CORRECTIONS

LIST No. ONE

Erroneous readings in the Hebrew Edition
(not eliminated in the English edition)

Among the erroneous readings in the book, the most common ones are the misreadings of י for ו (and *vice versa*).

The corrections are here arranged according to the pages; they are accompanied by bibliographical references and occasionally by short philological comments.

1) p. 8 l. 21 (חוקו) חוקוה read: (חיקו) חיקוה [see p. 183 l. 21].

2) p. 21 l. 5–6, the spelling שו does not appear in *IQS* but in *PH*. I prefer to read שיו [see *Lešonenu*, 35 (1971), p. 107 n. 25]. It is possible that the diphthong *aw* in the word שוא was contracted in Qumran, Hebrew; there is convincing evidence that final *aw* was pronounced *o* in the suffix יו- [see p. 447].

2*) p. 56 l. 11 (מסבּים), read: (מְסָבִּים).

3) p. 57 l. 9 יעקב, read: יעקוב.

4) p. 57 l. 15–16, in VII 21 the reading is יהיה = *MT*. Therefore this instance is not relevant.

5) p. 127 l. 25 רואנו, the ו is suspended after the א (see No. 26).

6) p. 128 l. 33, עשה does not appear in *DSW* VIII 7, but in *DSW* XI 7.

7) p. 132 l. 6, ידיחני does not appear in *DST* III 9, but in *DST* IV 8.

8) p. 132 l. 28, עץ in *PH* and *DST* XIV 24 is emended from עוץ.

9) p. 136 l. 3, אחשב *DST* VI 10, the correct reading is אֹתְחשב [see Kuhn, p. 78]. The exact reference is *DST* X 5.

10) p. 139 l. 2 חומצ IX 7, read: חומץ *DST* IV 11.

11) p. 139 l. 2 שורש IX 11, read: שורש *DST* IV 14 et al.

12) p. 139 l. 4 תכן, read: תרן.

13) p. 140 l. 10, מרודד is not found in *DSD* but in *DSW*.

14) p. 147 l. 5 רחבו *DSW* V 13, the correct reading is רוחבו.

15) p. 147 l. 11 טוהרה, first ה suspended.

16) p. 147 l. 8 לעבדך, read: וּלְעוֹבדָך.

17) p. 148 l. 1 חולינו, read: חוליינו (second י suspended).

18) p. 148 l. 25 שו, I give preference to the reading שיו [see supra 2].

19) p. 148 l. 26 ב[א]ון, read: בעוון [see Kuhn, p. 158].

20) p. 148 l. 26 הווות, or, may be, הריות?

21) p. 149 l. 26, לשת DST X 26 is from the root נשא rather than from the root שית.

22) p. 149 l. 38 תמשלוני, the ל is written on another letter, as Kutscher correctly observed, but in my opinion the deleted letter is ו rather than י. Hence the conjugation of this verb is *qal* rather than *hiph'il*.

23) p. 152 l. 34 שבה, read: שׁ'בה.

24) p. 154 l. 9 מעשוהו, read: מעשוהי (in both places) [see p. 213].

25) p. 154 l. 9 עושיהו, read: עושוהי (the second ו corrected from י) [see p. 532, last line].

26) p. 154 l. 10 רואינו (י suspended), the suspended letter is ו rather than י; so Kutscher also, on p. 526.

27) p. 154 l. 10 רעיהו (י suspended), the suspended letter is perhaps ו, and the scribe might have in mind the form רעוהי?

28) p. 154 l. 41 למיס, the correct reading is למוס, infinitive *qal* of מסס, [see Kuhn, p. 126].

29) p. 154 l. 42 [לה]מיס, a better suggestion is [לר]מוס [see Kuhn, p. 126].

30) p. 155 l. 9 כאיב the correct reading is כאוב, as Kutscher suggested on p. 376.

31) p. 155 l. 10 יעיף, the second י corrected from ס.

32) p. 155 l. 10 חשיכים, the correct reading is חשוכים, as Kutscher suggested on p. 155.

33) p. 155 l. 11, גזיל can also be read גזול [Loewinger, p. 142].

34) p. 155 l. 19–20, עיצה is עץ with a pronominal suffix and not עצה "council".

35) p. 155 l. 21 כאיב, also in DST, read: כאוב [see Qimron, *Waw* and *Yod* p. 110].

   Note: The readings suggested above (28–35) change the general picture concerning the use of י as a vowel letter designating long stressed ṣere.

36) p. 156 l. 31 ייטול, or perhaps ויטול? The first letter may be ו, as well as י. If so, we have here another example of a relative clause without a relative conjunction in MT, and a construction with ו conjunctive in the Scroll [see p. 431–432].

37) p. 156 l. 34 תיוסד (י suspended), in addition to Kutscher's suggestion one may also read יתוסד or יתיסד: the scribe might have changed the form from *niph'al* to *hithpa'el*.

38) p. 157 l. 22 קיצי, the צ is written on the י. The final reading is therefore קצי.

39) p. 157 l. 22, ויכנעים, the correct reading is נוכנעים, as Kutscher suggested (in brackets).

40) p. 157 l. 23 סיתאום, one should read סותאים [see RQ, 2 (1959/60), p. 552. Qimron, *Waw* and *Yod*, p. 110–111].

41) p. 157 l. 24 [תה[יל]ה], the reconstruction is unfounded; the י is not
visible in the photograph.

42) p. 157 l. 32 צידוק, the correct reading is צירוק [see Kuhn, p. 131 n. 4].
Note: The last 7 suggested readings (36–42) deal with the vowel letter
י representing a short i. Such spellings are extremely rare in the *DSS*.
As a matter of fact, there is hardly a couple of certain instances.

43) p. 158 l. 16 ותהיי, this reading is very doubtful. The second י seems
to be secondary; it is placed slightly above the line, and there is no space
between it and the ה of the word המשורה. Perhaps one should read:
ותהייה משורה?

44) p. 158 l. 17 ישתחוי, it seems that ישתחוו was originally ישתחוה (not
ישתחוי). (Compare also p. 532 l. 25: תשתחוו corrected from תשתחווה).

45) p. 159 l. 37 מצריי, the correct reading is מצריו [Loewinger, p. 142].

46) p. 160 l. 11 בטאטיי, both the reading and the meaning are doubtful.

47) p. 160 l. 26, add: תתיאמרו LXI 6.

48) p. 163 l. 26 נמנא, the א was apparently emended to ה.

49) p. 163 l. 32, add: קנאא LIX 17, כסה IX 13 (ה emended from א), חמה
XXXIV 2 (ה emended from א).

50) p. 165 l. 30 יואכולם, as a matter of fact the exact reading is ייאכולם.
The first י was added in the margin, but the second י was not changed
into ו. This form is of great importance for the problem of the imperfect with pronominal suffixes of the verb אכל [see p. 331].

51) p. 165 l. 36 יאכולוהו, read: יאכולוהי as in p. 213 l. 39.

52) p. 166 l. 39, in XXII 13 the reading is not צאן but צואן with a suspended ו.

53) p. 173 l. 21, אפו *DSD* II 9 is not אפוא but אפו [s. Kuhn, p. 21].

53*) p. 174 l. 7 או, read: וא.

54) p. 174 l. 12 שוו, this reading is very doubtful [see supra 1].

55) p. 175 l. 31 כאיב, the correct reading is כאוב [see supra 35].

56) p. 177 l. 20 נואם, read: לנואם.

57) p. 179 l. 27 [ג]לתיא, read: [גו]לתיא as in p. 370.

58) p. 182 l. 32, הרוה is not a good example for the spelling וה-, because
the two last letters, at least, represent corrections.

59) p. 185 l. 24, add: שעפי LVII 5.

60) p. 189 l. 13 ותשסילי, read: ותשפולי as in p. 330 l. 33.

61) p. 196 l. 29, Bab. כתובהא, as a matter of fact the form of the imperative
qal with the suffix ה- in the Babylonian tradition is *כותב֖הּ and not
*כתוב֖הּ.

62) p. 203 l. 3, add: לתוה (pronounced *lato*) XLIX 4. This form is of great
importance to the pronunciation of the word תהו and similar forms.

63) p. 207 l. 19, 22 ציין, [ש]בעין, these are not the only instances of ן in
the plural ending. First of all, the word ידין "hands" mentioned

in the Hebrew edition (see p. 473) is missing here. Apart from it, there are 4 words in which the ם (מ) of the plural ending seems to be a correction of ן: הדנים XIX 8, חמים XXIV 8, עריצים XXIX 5, המעמיקים XXIX 15.

64) p. 213 l. 11, add: ישתוהי 1XII 9.

65) p. 231 l. 27 f. בזאי, the ב is part of the word (and not a preposition) as shown from ל[ב]זאי נהרות DST VIII 14.

66) p. 288 l. 10 משימי, the corrected reading is משימו. In p. 560 l. 25 Kutscher reads: משומו [see Loewinger, p. 144].

67) p. 331 l. 24 ייעבורנו, the correct reading is יעובורנה (first ו suspended).

68) p. 331 l. 17, תנשו is not third person; hence it should be placed in the previous section.

69) p. 336 l. 32 jesbuleni, read: iezbuleni.

70) p. 340 l. 25 ייעבורנו, the correct reading is יעובורנה (first ו suspended).

71) p. 341 l. 25 יבחר, in xl 29 the correct reading is ובחר.

72) p. 341 l. 31 ישפול, the correct reading is ישפל. The line looking like ו is part of the ל.

73) p. 344 l. 2 יבזזו, the correct reading is ובזזו. There are no examples for the יבזזו type in Qumran. It is extremely rare in the Bible, and apparently fully absent from the good Manuscripts of the Mishna.

74) p. 353 l. 3 התקדשו, read: התקדישו.

75) p. 365 l. 26 אולמן, this word is only a reconstruction.

76) p. 379 l. 26 געים, the reading נועים is to be preferred [see RQ, 2 (1959/60), p. 234].

76*) p. 395 l. 3-8, the correct reading is והיית. Therefore this instance is not relevant.

77) p. 410 l. 19 = MT מיין, read: = MT יין.

78) p. 443 l. 27, 41 מאססוהי read: מאסטוהי.

79) p. 443 l. 33 מעשיהו, the correct reading is מעשוהי [see supra 24].

80) p. 443 l. 34 עושיהו, the correct reading is עושוהי [see supra 25].

81) p. 443 l. 36 ישתוהו, the correct reading is ישתוהי.

82) p. 445 l. 14 ועולוליהמה, read: ועילוליהמה as in p. 381 l. 14.

83) p. 447 l. 39–40, עיניהו etc. from DSD does not belong here. The suffix of these words is ־והי [Qimron, Waw and Yod p. 107].

84) p. 457 l. 7 קַרְסָלְי, read: קַרְסָלִי.

85) p. 459 l. 28 שלחי, read: שלחִי.

86) p. 463 l. 8 "u rather than i", read: "i rather than u".

87) p. 476 l. 24, the reading ביכורה is very doubtful [see p. 157].

88) p. 477 l. 1 יאכולוהו, the correct reading is יאכולוהי as in p. 213 l. 39.

89) p. 477 l. 5 יואכולם [see supra 50].

90) p. 480 l. 5 צְפַר (צְפַר in the English edition), read: צַפֵּר.

91) p. 480 l. 21, the reading בוהלה (suspended ו) is very doubtful. I prefer

to read בהלה without ו.

92) p. 498 l. 21 שריתו, read: שריתו.

93) p. 499 l. 2, 35 כאיב, read: כאוב [see supra 30].

94) p. 499 l. 18 סועלתם, Kutscher certainly had in mind the word סועלתמה LXV 7.

95) p. 500 l. 28, add the article of N. Berggrün, *Lešonenu*, 15 (1947), pp. 147–150.

96) p. 505 l. 16 קרתׄיכה, read: קרתיכה (the dots between the lines designate the Tetragrammaton).

97) p. 505 l. 22 שריתו, read: שריתו.

98) p. 505 l. 28 הדוש, read: הדש.

99) p. 506 l. 16, האזיִנ with suspended ה is also found in XXVIII 23 [see p. 526].

100) p. 508 l. 33: מנעצי֯ך. On the interchange of נעץ־נאץ see S. Lieberman, *Lešonenu*, XXXII (1967/68), p. 96–97.

101) p. 512 l. 6 חלינו (in the Hebrew edition חלייֹנו), the correct reading is חולייֹנו (second י suspended).

102) p. 527 l. 34 והוא (והיא in the English edition), read: והואה (first ו suspended).

103) p. 528 l. 9 רעיהו (suspended י), the suspended letter may also be ו [see supra 27].

104) p. 553 l. 42 באלוקי, read: באלקי.

105) p. 535 l. 10 ותמשלוני, in my opinion the original reading was ותמשולוני [see supra 22].

106) p. 560 l. 25 משומו, the correct reading is משימו [see supra 66].

LIST No. TWO

Corrections to the English Edition

p. VI l. 27 הז, read: הן.

p. VII l. 19 לול, read: לוא.

p. XIII l. 12 *archeology*, read: *Archaeology*.

    l. 31 *Lehaqurat*, read *Laḥaqirat*.

p. XIV l. 19 ־רד, read: ־ךד.

p. 3 l. 20 PNWM, read: PNMW.

p. 4 l. 9 ברכיה, זכריה, read: ברכיהו, זכריהו.

    l. 26 אושעיה, read: אושעיה.

    l. 33 נכיהו, read: נריהו.

p. 6 l. 16 יָפיו, read: יופיו.

    l. 20 צהובים, read: צהורים.

    l. 26 יטול, read: ייטול, but materially one can also read ויטול [see list 1 no. 36].

p. 10 l. 10 *Ta'anit'*, read: *Ta'anith*.

    l. 41 Pentacost, read: Pentecost.

p. 12 l. 7 *Ta'anit'*, read: *Ta'anith*.

p. 20 l. 4 לא = לוא, read: לא = לוא.

    l. 7 ראש for רואש, read: ראוש, רואש.

p. 21 l. 6 או, read: וא.

p. 22 l. 16 לנאם = לנואם, read: לנום = לנאם.

    l. 23 יבוה, read: בוה.

    Delete the word *and*.

    l. 28 cyprus, read: cypress.

p. 24 l. 13 No'aran, read: No'aran.

p. 25 l. 1 (superscript), read: (superscript ה).

p. 31 l. 24 בזחילו ורחיאו, read: בדחילו ורחימו.

    l. 26 at the beginning of the line, read: 'a watertight cistern' is...

p. 32 l. 2 לא יאירו, read: לוא יאירו.

    l. 15 חשיפי, read: חשופי.

p. 34 l. 19 עלכן, read: על כן.

    l. 22 יחמו, read: יחמול.

p. 35 l. 6 יתבטחו, read: ותבטחו.

    l. 22 translators, read: translator's.

p. 36 l. 14 after the word 'manner' read: ...אראלים ומצוקים אחזו ידן בלוחות הברית.

p. 39 l. 27 Galilaean, read: Galilean.

p. 41 l. 22 לרמס, read: לרמוס.

   l. 32, delete the word ניסוא.

   l. 33 עשר, read: עֶשָׂו.

p. 43 l. 6 בריתכמה, read: בריתכמה.

   l. 13 דבור, read: דיבור.

p. 44 l. 1 לשתותו ושמתיהו, read: ...ושמתיהו ...לשתותו

p. 47 l. 21 עלֿ, read: על.

   l. 22 ֿמנת, read: מנת.

p. 51 l. 16 אסרֿחדן, read: אסרחודן.

p. 52 l. 2–3 = , היאה, הואה, read: = . היאה, הואה

p. 53 l. 31 רְמוֹן, read: רִמּוֹן.

p. 54 l. 30 בֵּץ, read: בֵּ׳ץ.

p. 55 l. 11 פועל, read: פּועוּל.

p. 56 l. 10-11, read: As Prof. Z. Ben-Ḥayyim has shown, the form [כָּלָנוּ] מְסֻבִּים «are reclining» in the Passover *Haggadah* is a *hiph'il* form (מְסֻבִּים).

   l. 12 (השבט), read: "the tribe".

   l. 13 (השרביט), read: "the sceptre".

   l. 40, delete the word מוֹד.

p. 57 l. 10 (*Qere* *סורה?), read: (read: *סורה?).

   l. 11 *Qere* סולתי, read: read: סולתי.

   l. 15 יהיהי, read: יהיה.

   l. 15–16, delete all the words from יהיהי to יחיה

p. 58 l. 2 וֿעֿנין, read: וׂעינין.

p. 63 l. 7, add: אריה after the word 'word'.

   l. 14 קַרְסָלְי, read: קַרְסָלָי.

p. 64 l. 27 ֿיין = ֿין, read: יין = ין.

p. 66 l. 33 רִבִּי, read: רִבִּי.

   l. 45 רֶבֿֿרִבִּי, read: רֶבֿֿרֶבִּי.

p. 68 l. 7 קטל, read: קְטֵל.

p. 73 l. 39 יהיר, read: יהיה.

   ניתן read: נותן.

p. 80 l. 35 בעֿם, read: בעׂם.

   l. 38 יתיה, read: יתיב.

p. 81 l. 30 زعطوط, read: زعطوط .

p. 83 l. l. 6 scrolls other, read: other scrolls

p. 87 l. 30 *Kahane*, read: *Kahana*.

   l. 31, read: (Isa. XXXIV 7) ורדו ראמים עמם״ וא״ר מאיר וירדו רומים עמם ״ (vide *Tanḥuma*).

p. 89 l. 27 not true, read: true not.

l. 30, delete the word (Golgotha).

l. 43 גולגלתא, read: גולגולתא.

p. 90 l. 15, 34 Beni Ḥazir, read: *B^enē Ḥēzīr*.

p. 92 l. 34 רא־בי־י, read: ראב־י־.

p. 93 l. 7 delete מבית שאן.

p. 96 l. 35 בעל שמון, in the Hebrew edition: בעלשמן.

p. 103 l. 20 Χελικίου, in the Hebrew edition Χελκίου

p. 103 l. 36 אר, הור, הר, read: הור, הר, אר.

p. 105 l. 29 ישיאמל, read: ישים אל.

p. 107 l. 2 יורשלם, read: ירושלם.

p. 110 l. 17 הֻטֵל, read: קֻטֵל.

p. 112 l. 29 שטים, read: שמים.

p. 114 l. 31 בָּצְרָה, read: בָּצְרָה.

p. 118 l. 15 רומליהו, read: רומליה.

p. 119 l. 10 ריצון, read: דיצון.

l. 26 דצין, read: קצין.

p. 121 l. 5–6, read: it appears that שבנא is an abbreviation of the name שבניהו־שבניה.

l. 39–40, read: שבניהו, שבניו, שבניה, שבני, שבנא.

p. 127 l. 2 Yellin, read: Yalon.

l. 8 מששה, read: משאה.

p. 128 l. 31 קטע, read: fragment.

p. 139 l. 9 ־אותות, read: insignia.

p. 143 l. 8 שורשם, this form does not exist in *1QIs*^a.

p. 143 l. 24 חטד, read: חטר.

l. 42 in *DSW*... read: in *DSW* XIV 7 we find מתנים and in *DST* X 33 מותני !

p. 144 l. 6, delete the word twice (after גדל).

p. 147 l. 28–29, the correct reading is אשקיטה. Therefore it is not in place here.

p. 148 l. 13 נוערן, read: No'aran.

p. 149 l. 20 וורגו, read: יירגו.

p. 149 l. 41 ישקימו, read: ישפיקו.

p. 152 l. 26 *PH* IV 4, read: *PH* IV 7.

p. 153 l. 5 גיזברק, read: גיזברה.

l. 10 ביצים, read: "eggs".

p. 155 l. 10, after the word חשכים, read: L 10.

p. 156 l. 26 ונישאום, read: תישאום.

p. 158 l. 2 בשבמך, read: בשבתך.

p. 161 l. 27, instead of החזן, read: "the sexton".

l. 28 Piqwhich, read: Piq which.

l. 29, instead of הדיין, read: "the judge".

ריאנא, read: דיאנא.

p. 163 l. 25, instead of p. 244 read: p. 284.

p. 164 l. 39 קורד, read: קורה.

p. 165 l. 19 תיאמרו, read: תואמרו.

p. 165 l. 36, before IV 1 add: נאכל.

p. 166 l. 30 ראשכים, read: ראשיכם.

p. 170 l. 17 *wav*, read *waw*.

p. 171 l. 2 שמוורים, read: שמורים.

    l. 28 ליא אתה, the א of ליא is suspended.

p. 175 l. 10, instead of II 6 b read: II b 6.

p. 183 l. 21, add: אותוה XXXVI 21.

p. 185 l. 30 Samar. Bible, read: Samar. Pentateuch.

p. 187 l. 27 SP, read: Samar. Pentateuch.

p. 194 l. 12 עיבדו, read: עיברו (suspended י [?]).

    l. 22 by, read: with.

p. 195 l. 5-7, read: have been facilitated by the fact that the pausal forms of Standard Hebrew (which I take to be more or less the same as *MT*) are identical to the Aramaic forms.

    l. 17 are pausal, reads: are not pausal.

    l. 38 אבהו, read: אהָבוּ.

    l. 42 צעו, read: דעו.

p. 196 l. 12 שמרם, read: שׁמֹרם.

p. 199 l. 25 ויהבינהו *DSD* VI, read: ויהבינהו (suspended ה) *DSD* VI 15.

p. 199 l. 37 הבינהו, read: ויהבינהו (suspended ה) *DSD* VI 15. The original reading was ולבינהו, and it was emended to והבינהו or ויהבינהו [see Kuhn p. 31].

p. 201 l. 17, delete the vocalization of the word וברכים.

    l. 31 141 i, read: 141 e. not, read: note.

    l. 33 Galilean, read: Galilean Aramaic.

p. 203 l. 6 *DWS*, read: *DSW*.

    l. 30, I 10, read: L 10.

p. 209 l. 2 *Thal*, read: J. Theodor and Ch. Albeck.

    l. 25 רעתך, read: דעתך.

p. 210 l. 6, the words בנותיך ... שוממותיך, חרבותיך of the Hebrew edition were omitted.

p. 211 l. 37 Ginzberg, read: Ginsberg.

p. 213 l. 27–28, read: אל תיראי תולעת יעקוב... אני עזרתיכה (עזרתיך *MT*) וגואלכה... (וגואלך *MT*) XLI 14.

p. 214 l. 6, delete the number II after *DSD*.

p. 217 l. 26 אפעל, read: אוחד.

p. 220 l. 10, read: (the three last words are superscript) ואספה פליטת בית יהודה... *MT* = ריספה (הנשארה) והנמצא *MT* =) שורש למטה.

p. 223 l. 4 Zoan, read: צען.

l. 7 למהבת, read: ‏.למבהת

l. 19 בחן = בחר, read: ‏.בחן = בחר

p. 226 l. 20 צוין, read: ‏.ציון

p. 227 l. 30 רוש, read: ‏.דוש

l. 31 גרן, read: ‏.גדר

גדר, read: ‏.גרן

p. 228 l. 12 *daijoth*, read: *dajoth*.

p. 229 l. 4 דֵעו, read: ‏.דֵעי

l. 9 לבעיד, read: ‏.לבער

l. 14 מצריי, read: ‏.מצריו

l. 19 הוא, read: ‏.אוה

On pp. 231-291 there are some 30 Hebrew explanatory phrases, which were either not translated into English or were translated but remained adjacent to the English translation. Since this is a common feature of the book and cannot lead to misunderstanding they have not been included.

p. 234 l. 17 ״אין, read: ‏.אין

l. 18 ״אדם, read: ‏.אדם

p. 235 l. 41 כלה =, read: "bride".

p. 237 l. 30, transliteration, read: sound change.

p. 238 l. 35 אדמתה, read: ‏.אדמתא

p. 239 l. 12 חרש (ברזל מעצד), read: ‏.חרש (ברזל מעצד)

חרש(עצים), read: ‏.חרש (עצים)

p. 240 l. 21 instead of חששה being = to ששׁ + Aram. def. art., read: חששה = ששׁ + Aram. def. art.

p. 241 l. 2 ‏...‏תבאש, read: ‏...‏תבאש

l. 6 אשים מדבר ...אחריב, read: ‏.אחריב... אשים

p. 243 l. 16 חלבנים, read: ‏.הלבנים

p. 247 l. 3-4, delete the word (כבש שעבד, לעבד).

l. 7 Qamez, read: Qameṣ.

p. 248 l. 17 חָדל, read: ‏.חָדל

p. 248 l. 28-29, (both variations of the word לאות), read: (both mean 'weary-ness').

p. 248 l. 33 כליון =, read: = 'destruction'.

p. 250 l. 33 לאכן, read: ‏.לא כן

p. 251 l. 1 בדיץ, read: ‏.בדיו

p. 253 l. 34 עד עאדוהי, read: ‏.עדעאדוהי

p. 254 l. 13 ממקרמו, read: ‏.ממקומו

p. 255 l. 17 מחץ, read: ‏.מחֵץ

l. 25, instead of דרש, read: homiletical interpretation.

p. 260 l. 5, read: ‏.מצדה – מצרה, מצְרת – מצודות

l. 17 מצורח, read: ‏.מצורה

p. 261 l. 2 emend., read: edition.

p. 262 l. 37, Hanman, read: Haneman.

p. 265 l. 36, *DSD* Qumran I ii 5, read: *Sa* II 5 (= *DJD*, I, p. 110).

p. 266 l. 35 צאן, read: צען.

    l. 36, delete the word חטעות.

p. 267 l. 7 חנשה לי, read: תנשה לי.

p. 269 l. 20, infinitive in the absolute state, read: infinitive absolute.

p. 278 l. 26 σαυλασαν, read: σαυλασαυ.

    l. 31 צייו, read: ציין.

p. 280 l. 1 יצריחו, read: יצריחו.

p. 282 l. 6 מצורה – מצודות, read: מצרת – מצודות.

p. 286 l. 22 ירים, read: ירום.

    l. 31 הרעיו, read: הריעו.

p. 287 l. 8 הפחצבת, read: המחצבת.

p. 288 l. 21 ושמלחנו, read: ושמלתנו.

p. 289 l. 13 חרס, read: הרס.

p. 290 l. 11 ירקדנא, read: יוקדנא.

    l. 30 לְהַשׁוֹת, read: לְהַשּׁוֹת.

p. 291 l. 26 לחשתחות, read: להשתחות.

p. 293 l. 6 תתע, read: תֹּתע.

p. 294 l. 10 מאות נפש, read: תאות נפש.

p. 295 l. 7 שדוינא, read: שרוינא.

    l. 14, delete the words זכר ("masc.").

    l. 21, read: אורח.

p. 296 l. 27, Qere, read: read.

    l. 28, Qere, read: read.

    l. 41, Qere, read: reading.

p. 306 l. 8, 44%, read: 40%.

    l. 10, 2.5%, read: 52.5%.

    l. 12, 8.5%, read: 58.5%.

p. 309 l. 16, delete the word superior.

p. 313 l. 40, after the word language, add: influence.

p. 315 l. 18, Lawinger, read: Loewinger.

    l. 32 ~(בתן) ברח~, read: ~(בתן) ברח~.

p. 316 l. 20 חים, read: חיה.

p. 318 l. 20, I 2, read: L 2.

p. 320 l. 26 אותבי, read: אוהבי.

    l. 38 ...גבהו, read: כי גבהו...

    l. 39 כניבה, read: כְּנִבָה.

p. 322 l. 22 כהוא, read: כהנא.

    l. 26 פֶּקְדָה, read: פְּקָדָה.

p. 323 l. 13 קרה, read: קרובה.

p. 325 l. 22 רָאתִין, read: וְרָאתִין.

p. 330 l. 23, imperal, read: imperfect.

p. 331 l. 1 תֵאָמֵנוּ, read: תֵאָמֵינוּ.

l. 27 יאכולוהו, read: יאכולוהי.

p. 333 l. 29 יעבדוכי, read: יעבודוכי.

l. 32, read: but the matter cannot be treated at length here.

p. 336 l. 37 יקטְלוּ, read: יֶקְטְלוּ.

p. 341 l. 21 יאכולוהו, read: יאכולוהי.

l. 38 קַט, read: קְטַל.

p. 344 l. 20, in the ם of the root, read: after the נ.

p. 348 l. 8 מבוח, read: טבוח.

l. 11 גובח, read: גובה.

p. 350 l. 15 חולו, read: חולי.

p. 353 l. 3 התקדישו, read: התקדישו.

l. 38, (the last word), read: ועמודו.

p. 354 l. 14 וילד, read: יולד.

p. 357 l. 28 ושאן, read: ישאן.

l. 37, Sch., read: Scr.

p. 361 l. 32 קדוב ה׳, read: קדוש ה׳.

p. 373 l. 18, Löw, read: Lowe.

l. 30, medial, read: instrumental.

p. 375 l. 10 קטְל, read: קְטַל.

p. 377 l. 8 להבה (להבות) אש להבה, read: אש להבה (להבות).

p. 378 l. 31, interprets, read: homiletical interpretation.

p. 386 l. 17 תבלות – תבלית, read: תבלית – תבלות.

l. 26 to p. 387, l. 4: many mistakes occurred in the figures; the whole section, in its corrected form, is reprinted, here, as follows:

"Of the 72 words which have been discussed in this section, making a total of 83 cases, we find the following:

1) *MT* is superior[2] in 30 words, which make 32 instances (7 of which are doubtful). This is 41.5% of the cases; numbers 4, 6, 16, 17, 18, 19, 20, 21(?), 22, 23, 24, 24a, 24b(?), 28(?), 29, 35, 38 (*bis, vide infra* 3), 39, 41(?), 45(?), 49, 54, 55, 58(?), 59, 61, 62, 66, 68, 70.

2) Scr. is superior in 7 words, which make 11 cases (5 of which are doubtful), i.e. 9.5% numbers 13, 25, 26(?), 40, 60, (? 4 times), 64, 67 (*vide infra* 3).

3) Non-determinable Forms: 35 words, which make 40 instances; numbers 1, 2 (*bis*), 3, 5, 7, 8, 9, 10, 11, 12, 14, 15, 26, 30, 31, 32, 33, 34, 36 (*bis*), 37, 38 (*vide supra* 1), 42, 43, 44, 46, 47, 48, 50, 51, 52, 53 (three times), 56, 57, 63, 65, 67 (*vide supra* 2), 69".

p. 389 l. 16, Horowitz, read: Hurvitz.

p. 392 l. 5–6, read: קום (superscript *yod*, ph.) ולוא תיסיף (subject = הארץ) ונפל.

    l. 16–17, there should be no space between the two lines.

    l. 21 וקראת, read: וְקָרָאת.

    l. 26 כסא, read: כסה.

    l. 36, read: (Ketib = בחיניו, Qere).

p. 393 l. 38 ימצאו, read: ומצאו.

    l. 39 לילת, read: לילית.

p. 394 l. 29 accordingly and, read: and accordingly.

    l. 36 ועצמותיכח, read: ועצמותיכה (suspended ה).

    l. 40 Mishna, read: *Mishnah*.

p. 395 l. 27 התערבנא, read: התערב נא .

p. 398 l. 16 שני = סביר !, read: שנים *sevirin*: שני.

    l. 17, common, read: collective.

p. 399 l. 35 הזכירוני. This word is mentioned twice: here and on p. 398 l. 31.

p. 400 l. 21, delete the word 'am.

p. 403 l. 34, *Haketuvot*, read: *Haketovot*.

p. 404 l. 4 ה, read: + ה.

p. 405 l. 29 בחוק, read: בחזק (suspended ב).

p. 414–429 ו copula, read: *waw* conjunctive.

p. 422 l. 7, in B, read: in the following list (2).

    l. 10 disappers, read: disappears.

p. 429 l. 5, not about, read: about.

p. 431 l. 22 משבט, read: בשבט.

p. 434 l. 35 הן, read: הם.

p. 441 l. 29, Masorah, read: tradition.

p. 443 l. 17 אלוהוא, read: אלוהו.

p. 445 l. 9 עשיתם, read: עשיתים.

p. 446 l. 40 ה -ת, read: -ה, -ת.

p. 447 l. 12 בראושיו, read: ברואשיו.

    l. 26 מאססוהו, read: ומאססוהי.

p. 448 l. 2, Versions etc., read: traditions of Hebrew.

    l. 11, Masorah, read: tradition.

    l. 24 י-כמה, read: -יכמה.

p. 449 l. 12, Masora, read: tradition.

    l. 18, Masorah, read: tradition.

p. 450 l. 8, particles, read: short words.

p. 451 l. 32 עורסכה, read: עורסדה.

    l. 33 כסיכסה, read: כסיכמה.

p. 453 l. 16 כָּתֹנֶת, read: כְּתֹנֶת.

    l. 17 שָׁבֹּלֶת, read: שַׁבֹּלֶת.

    l. 19 כִּתָן, read כִּתָן.

    l. 27 רְמֹן, read: רִמֹון.

p. 455 l. 6 כְּתֹנֶת, read: כְּתֹנֶת.

p. 456 l. 4, Harwitz, read: Hurvitz.

l. 12, *shulma-nu*, read: *shulma:nu*.

l. 13, *purshu'u*, read: *purshu'u*.

l. 14, *parshu'u*, read: *parshu'u*.

p. 458 l. 8, read: אֹמֶר – אָמְרֵי – אִמְרוּ.

p. 458 l. 16 רַחֲבָה, read: רַחֲבָה.

l. 22 سوقم , read: تُفَل .

l. 24 אֳהָבִים, read: אֳהָבִים.

p. 459 l. 11 שטטין, read: שיטין.

l. 20 בְּסֹרוּ, read: בָּסֹרוּ.

l. 24 ישרחו, read: ישרהו.

l. 27 שָֽׁעֲלוּ, read: שָׁעֲלוּ.

שָׁעֲלוּ, read: שָׁעֲלוּ.

l. 31 ברכיא ?, read: בוכיא ?

l. 42 גְּבַל, read: גְּבַל.

p. 460 l. 8, Masorah, read: tradition.

l. 10, Masorah, read: tradition.

p. 461 l. 3, Masorah, read: tradition.

l. 5, Masorah, read: tradition.

l. 14, Masorah, read: tradition.

l. 20 אחליאב, read: אהליאב.

l. 22 נעמי, read: נָעֳמִי.

p. 462 l. 17 גבה, read: גֹּבַה.

l. 30 משושה, read: מְשׁוּכָה.

p. 463 l. 4 משטה, read: מְשָׂטָה.

משושה, read: מְשׁוּטָה.

l. 12 ברסדי, read: בְּרָדִים.

p. 464 l. 21 קֽטְלוּ, read: קָטְלוּ.

l. 25, Masorah, read: tradition.

l. 31 קָרֲבָה, read: קָרֲבָה.

p. 465 l. 1 נערה, read: נִצְרָה.

l. 7 קטל, read: קטן.

l. 10, Masorah, read: tradition.

l. 11, Masorah, read: tradition.

l. 34 לחוינגה, read: לחונה.

p. 466 l. 10 הפציל, read: הפעיל.

l. 12, Masorah, read: tradition.

l. 16 יטחו, read: יָסְחוּ.

p. 467 l. 31, Masorah, read: tradition.

p. 468 l. 23 קֽטֵל, read: קָטֵל.

p. 468 l. 39 מהלה, read: מְקָלָה.

p. 469 l. 5 הוסעל, read: הוּסְעַל.

    l. 16 חיצדך, read: חיצן.

    l. 19, Gitiymunima, read: *Gitirimunima*.

    l. 28 קטל, read: קַטְלָן.

p. 471 l. 2, conjugated, read: declined.

    l. 5, conjugation, read: pattern.

        unconjugated, read: undeclined.

p. 471 l. 12 קטל, read: קְטֵל.

p. 472 l. 4 (יֶלֶד)לד(*), read: לד (יֶלֶד).

p. 473 l. 6 יעבצ, read: יעבֵּץ.

    l. 14 أس , read: أمس .

p. 474 l. 38 ראשן, read: ראשון.

p. 475 l. 11 קטיל, read: קְטֵל.

    l. 26 קְטָלָה, read: קְטָלָא.

    l. 35, primary, read: following.

    l. 41 שיליח, read: שִׁילַח.

    l. 42 גיחן, read: גיחון.

p. 476 l. 9 קסוק – קוסד, read: קסוד – קוסד.

    l. 10 צודוק, the correct reading is צירוק (see list 1 No. 42).

    l. 11, Part., read: Fragment.

    l. 26, conjugated, read: declined.

    l. 27, conjugated, read: declined.

    l. 30 נכוחות, read: נכחות.

        נכחות, read: נכחות.

p. 477 l. 22 שוחי׳, read: שוחי.

    l. 23 שחי, read: שְׁחִי.

    l. 38 רְנִי, read: רַנִּי.

p. 478 l. 10 אמריכמה, read: אמריכמה.

    l. 20 הק, read: חק.

        conjugated, read: declined.

    l. 36 טסרוחי, read: טסרוהי.

        (צסרין-), read (fingernails).

        (also קְטָל, also read: קְטָל),.

p. 479 l. 9 כותנא, read: כותינא.

        נימום, read: נימוס.

    l. 19 בתמתא, read: בטמתא.

        in Palestine, read: in Jewish Aramaic.

    l. 28 قُرْن read: قَرُب .

p. 480 l. 1, in Palestine, read: in Jewish Aramaic.

    l. 1, 8 צְפַר, read: צֶפַר.

    l. 10 צֶפַר, read: צָפַר.

l. 11 קוסד - , read: קוסד.

l. 23 כבוד, read: הכבד.

l. 24, *xənər*, read: *xənṣər*.

l. 32, p. 41 *himmasi*, read: p. 141 *himmaṣ*.

p. 481 l. 4, tradition, read: version.

l. 8 נימום, read: נימוס.

l. 27, read: "*Leshon Ḥakhamim — Ma Tiva?*".

l. 30–31, footnote 4, read: The vocalizations in the *Mishna*: *Kil'ayim*: יחור Kaufmann ms.; יֵחוּר Parma ms. *Orla*: יְחוּר Kaufmann ms.; יָחוּר Parma ms. Were it not...

p. 482 l. 6 קבָּה, read: חבָּה.

l. 7 פְטָמָה, read: פְטְמָה.

l. 34 תורער, read: תורעה.

p. 483 l. 3 (- youth), read: "young".

l. 4 גיחיר, read: גיחור.

l. 23 *a:n*, read: +*a:n*.

l. 35 Is also, read: קולחא is also.

l. 42 זוירין, read: מזירין.

p. 484 l. 5 in the Scr., read: like the Scr.

l. 16 שורויא, read: שורויה.

l. 17 - התחלתו, read: "his beginning".

l. 21 *חרות, read: חרות.
חירית, read: חירות.

l. 23 חיר-ה, read: חירייה.
חור-ה, read: חורייה.'

l. 26 יביד, read: יבוד.

p. 485 l. 2 טוכיא, read: סוכיא.

l. 8 חודיא, read: חודוא.

l. 9 שיקרא, read: שוקרא.

p. 486 l. 22 צפֶר, read: צפֵר.

l. 26 نَقب , read: نَقَب .

p. 487 l. 1 נקיב, read: נְקב.

l. 13–14, Bib. Hebr. Tiberian, read: Tiberian Bib. Hebrew.

l. 14 כֻּתֹּנֶת, read: כֻּתֹּנֶת.
צפֹּר, read: צפֹּר.

l. 15 כְּתֹנֶת, read: כֻּתֹּנֶת.

l. 18 צֶפֶר, read: צֵפֶר.

p. 488 l. 4 حله , read: حكه .

l. 7 قسط , read: قَسط .

l. 15 سنرر , read: سنور .

l. 17 قنديد , read: قنليد .

p. 488 l. 17 مصطار , read: مُصطار .

l. 18 علیـه , read: عُلیـه .

l. 20 حـلـه , read: حُـلـه .

p. 490 l. 13, *subh*, read: *ṣubḥ*.

p. 491 l. 31, 'Usifya, read: *'Usufia*.

p. 493 l. 37 'יוונה, read: יוונה.

p. 495 l. 24 *ʔima:la*, read: *'ima:la*.

p. 496 l. 3 Aramaic influence, read: Aramaic substratum influence.

l. 38 גברוא = גברייא, read: גּבְרוֹא = גּבְרֵיָא.

p. 497 l. 1 in Samaritan, read: in Samaritan Aramaic.

l. 2 Galilean, read: in Galilean Aramaic and.

l. 7 read: in Galilean Aramaic מוגדליא, מוגדלא = מגדליא = מגדלא (place name) מגדליא

l. 16 רומליהו, read: רומליה.

l. 35 שיביט, read: שרביט.

p. 498 l. 6 Samaritan, read: Samaritan Aramaic.

l. 10 Samaritan, read: Samaritan Aramaic.

שמוכן = *שומכן = שומיכן, read: *שמיכן

l. 20 שיריתו, read: שריתו.

l. 37 שומירון, read: שומיכן.

שמירון, read: שמיכן.

תימנין, read: תומנין.

l. 39, *lehaqurat*, read: *laḥaqirat*.

p. 499 l. 3 ואום, read: נאום.

p. 500 l. 2 Galilean, read: Galilean Aramaic.

l. 3 שמרות, read: שמחת.

l. 14 Samaritan, read: Samaritan Aramaic.

she':l, read: *she'o:l*.

l. 23 סרדום, read: סודם.

l. 43 the verb appears here as חלום, read: The vowel of the second syllable is o.

p. 501 l. 9 שביזית[4], read: שביזית.

l. 11 column, read: column[4].

p. 502 l. 21 אודן, read: אוזן.

l. 22 יושר (suspended *waw*) אמתכמה, read: ישור אמתכה.

p. 503 l. 11 חוטור (the second), read: חוטיר.

l. 23 יושור (suspended *waw*) אמתכה, read: ישור אמתכה.

p. 504 l. 23 גמֶר, read: גְמֶר.

p. 505 l. 14 תנתיו, read: תנתו.

l. 16 תנשאנה, read: תנשאנה.

l. 20 הצא°צאים, read: הצא°צאים.

p. 506 l. 11 להשאוות, read: לשאוות.

l. 21 הילילי, read: הילילו.

l. 22 אדם, read: אדס.

l. 25, transfer the word תחלתי to line 30.

l. 29 ונחלם, read: ינחלם

l. 31 עמסום, read: עמסים

l. 34 המסום, read: המסים

p. 507 l. 6 ואלו יהיה, read: but יהיה.

l. 33 יונדע, read: ונודע.

p. 508 l. 18 ציאונו, read: צואונו (first *waw* suspended; second *waw* erased).

p. 509 l. 16 משעיק, read: משעיך.

l. 34 וצרחי, read: יצרחי.

l. 30, Samaritan, read: Samaritan Aramaic.

l. 36 תומוה, read: תומיה.

p. 510 l. 2 עסוקה, read: עסיקה.

l. 12, Samaritan, read: Samaritan Aramaic.

l. 14, Galilean, read: Galilean Aramaic.

l. 16, Aramaic, read: Arabic.

p. 511 l. 10. תזכר (the second), read: תזכור.

l. 32, read: A. j, jj near e: , i: - '.

p. 512 l. 31 צָיִים, read: צִיִּים.

p. 513 l. 13 אועיה, read: גועיה.

l. 15 *אואין, read: *גואין.

l. 25 תחויה, read: החויה.

p. 514 l. 3, plethora, read: plural.

יקודי, read: יהודי.

l. 5, delete: ערביים *et sim.* In gentilica.

l. 16 והודים, read: יהודים.

l. 36 לניים, read: לויים.

p. 515 l. 12 Pesher Nachum, read: *Pesher Naḥum.*

l. 22, In Arabic..., read: In Arabic one find فِطِّيس and فِنْطِيس.

l. 23, *Fantis/flantis?, read: •פנטיש and פלטיש•?.

l. 34, p. 176 מצרײם, read: מצרײם p. 176.

p. 516 l. 2 יודינו, read: יודינו.

l. 15, Samaritan, read: Samaritan Aramaic.

l. 29 נדיאל, read: דניאל.

l. 30 גחואה, read: החואה.

l. 44 ייהלא רתנה , read: הלא יירתנה.

p. 517 l. 3 נהת, read: נחת.

l. 34 עודות, read: עידות.

עודוד, read: עידוד.

p. 519 l. 19, instead of המגילה לקתה כאן בחסר, read: The Scroll is lacking here.

l. 28 עשוא, read: עשו.

l. 33 *vide*, read: (*vide.*

l. 38–39, delete the two lines.

p. 520 l. 3, instead of ?(ph.) שׁט, read: (*waw* corrected from *yod*).

l. 8, read: עירים (BH *Ketib* and *Qere*).

l. 30 ינצירי, read: ונצירי.

l. 31 וסצחו (in the *Ketib* column), read: יסצחו.

p. 521 l. 29 התיר, read: התיו.

l. 30–33 תסימו, read: תוסימו *Ketib*, תוסימי *Qere* (according to Gins-burg תוסימו *Qere*. He does not mention *Madinḥa'e*).

p. 521 l. 36 קומי, read: קומי.

l. 38 ויסלח, read: ויסרח.

p. 522 l. 9 ונהריך, read: ונהרתיך.

l. 13 יצורך, read: יוצרך.

l. 26 ואשרכם, read: ואשכרם.

l. 29 יל, read: על.

p. 523 l. 1 ורו ממתי, read: ורוממתי.

l. 8 בי, read: בין.

l. 9 כא, read: כ'א.

l. 20, ṣade, read: ṣade?

l. 27 ובח'ר, read: ובח'ור.

l. 28 תעז'ב, read: תעל'ב.

p. 524 l. 1 האבת, read: האבות.

l. 2 וי״ו?, read: *waw*?

l. 12 המל, read: חמל.

l. 23 (מחוקה), read: (erased).

l. 24 ירבצו, read: ירבְצו.

l. 32 יוליליי, read: היוליליי (suspended ו). In my opinion the correct reading is הילילי. The line looking like *waw* is the head of a *lamed*.

p. 527 l. 4 לו אᵃדם, read: לואᵃדם.

l. 20 יעובורנו, read: יעוברנה.

l. 23 הדבים, read: הדברים.

p. 528 l. 13 נס'כהמה, read: נס'כהמה.

נסיך, read: נסיך.

p. 529 l. 9, Scr., read: MT.

l. 10 וסדרו(וי, read: וסדרוי'י (second ו suspended).

p. 531 l. 23 מל'ד, read: מל'ד.

p. 532 l. 2 לᵊעמיס, read: לעמים.

l. 3 לᵊערוץ, read: לערוץ.

l. 21 כל, read: כל;

l. 24 יחכיתי, read: וחכיתי.

l. 33, read: ציון (erased) בת (suspended) יושבת = MT...

p. 533 l. 2 *qaf*, read: *qof*.

l. 15 יעיטך? ועטך? read: ועוטך? יעוטך?

l. 30 ובלשן, read: ובלשן.

p. 534 l. 6 יזם, read: זרם.

l. 33 עצתן, read: עצתו.

p. 535 l. 6 עמסות, read: עמוסות.

l. 19 בתסרב, read: בלחרב.

l. 24, *qaf*, read: *qof*.

l. 27 רוברך, read: רוביך (suspended י).

l. 41 האריכי, read: האיריכי.

p. 536 l. 8 בעוין, read: בעוון.

l. 36, XLIX, read: LIX.

l. 37 ואצבעותיכמה, read: ואצבעותיכמה.

p. 527 l. 7 עלו, read: עשו.

l. 38 פיששם, read: פ.שם.

p. 539 l. 1, versions, read: readings.

l. 42 מלד, read: מלך.

p. 540 l. 24 ושבת כה, read: ושבתכה.

l. 34 עלות, read: עלית.

l. 38 עישה, read: עשה.

p. 541 l. 9 נכתין, read: נכתי.

l. 27 אתשיתי, read: אחשיתי.

l. 41 גרוליו, read: גחליו.

p. 543 l. 5 וקרא, read: יקרא.

אלקי, read: אלוקי.

l. 12 אלקיך, read: אלוקיך.

l. 25 יועילוך, read: יועילוך...

p. 544 l. 7, version, read: readings.

l. 12, read: נצר מטעי = MT (ph.) הריה מעשי ידיו (*Ketib* מטעו, *Qere* נצר מטעי).

l. 16 יועד, read: ועד.

l. 24, read: קודשי = MT (suspended *waw*) אמר אלוקיך...

p. 545 l. 11 Students of Bible, read: Biblical scholars.

l. 34 אלקיך, read: אלוקיך.

p. 547 l. 21 ועוני, read: ועיני.

p. 548 l. 40 אשור את עדבדו, read: ועבדו את אשור.

p. 549 l. 12 שנח, read: שנה.

l. 13 ההום, read: ההוא.

p. 550 l. 16 the word, read: the word שמה.

l. 20 ושבנה, read: ושבנא.

l. 35 homoeoteleuson?, read: homoeoteleuton?

p. 551 l. 3 כארץ, read: בארץ.

l. 36 תצמוח, read: תצמיח.

l. 41 קרוש, read: קדוש.

p. 552 l. 24 והילילו, read: יהילילו.

l. 41 גדור..., read: גדול (suspended) (גדיל?) יתר מואד.

p. 553 l. 3 ואנחתו, read: ואנחהו.

l. 21 לחבש (the second), read: ולחבש.

l. 42, read: = Scr. (space of half a line) והמיתכה אדנות הויה תמיד

p. 554 l. 1 יהנשבע, read: והנשבע.

l. 6 אמר, read: ...אמר.

p. 555 l. 27 אליהם, read: להמה.

l. 38 בלתך, read: דבלת.

p. 556 l. 9 is in, read: is rare in.

l. 14 יקום לעילם, read: יקום לעולם.

l. 15–16, these two lines are completely disturbed.

l. 27 יוחנו, read: יודינו, more exactly יודינו.

גורים, read: גואים.

l. 30–31, there should be no space between the two lines.

p. 557 l. 38 וזמרתיח, read: וזמרתיה.

p. 558 l. 17 אהרא, read: אהרון.

l. 26, read: = Scr. סריה (apparently corrected from בטעפיה) בטעפי.

l. 38 סדה, read: יסדָה.

p. 559 l. 3 ושועתך, read: ישועתך.

l. 16, read: זרם (erasure dots before the *mem*) וסתר:ם.

l. 21 כיה, read: כיא.

p. 560 l. 14, read: = Scr. ...יוציא(ph.) ומשפסטו.

l. 17 הביאו, read: ...הביאו.

l. 20 יעמיעוכם, read: ישמיעוכם.

l. 25 משומו (the first), read: משומי. About the second משומו, see list 1 No. 66.

l. 27 ותארהו, read: יתארהו.

l. 38 וצרתיה, read: יצרתיה.

p. 561 l. 8 הביאותיהו, read: והביאותיהו.

l. 15 קדשו, read: קדושו.

l. 19 זרועי, read: זרעי.

l. 20 אליו, read: ...אליו.

l. 25 ינחמן, read: ינחמך.

l. 32 חשבנוחי, read: חשבנוהי.

ולא, read: ולוא.

p. 562 l. 5 אשכין, read: אשכן.

ושכן, read: ישכן.

l. 7 לבו (the second), read: לבי.

l. 17, read: (Ketib מטעו, Qere) מטעי.

l. 25 כמהל, read: לכמה.

p. 563 l. 17, versions, read: readings.

    l. 28 גאין, read: גאון (twice).

    l. 35 הגנו, read: הגני.

p. 564 l. 2 ונתתו, read: ונתתי.

    l. 7 מלקח, read: מלקוח.

    l. 8 ומלט, read: ימלט.

    l. 17 בארעם, read: בארצם.

p. 565 l. 32 נה־, read: ־כה.

p. 566 l. 10 Bible, read: Pentateuch.

    l. 15 האוינה, read: האזינה.

    l. 16 ראישן, read: ראישון.

    l. 18 העצרה, read: עצרתה.

    l. 19 חבדילתי, read: הבדילתי.

Printed in the United States
by Baker & Taylor Publisher Services